★ Belo Horizonte

M I N A S

G E R A I S

Serra da Mantiqueira

Paraíba do Sul

19

22

21

2   12

3   6   5

10 7   8

13   9   1   R I O   D E

4

16   15   *Serra do Mar*   J A N E I R O

17   ★ Rio de Janeiro

★ São Paulo

O

L   O

A T L A N T I C   O C E A N

N

0 10 20 30 40 miles

0 10 20 30 40 km

FAZENDAS

THE GREAT HOUSES AND PLANTATIONS OF BRAZIL

FAZENDAS

THE GREAT HOUSES AND PLANTATIONS OF BRAZIL

FERNANDO TASSO FRAGOSO PIRES

PHOTOGRAPHS BY NICOLAS SAPIEHA

TRANSLATED FROM THE PORTUGUESE BY
GREGORY RABASSA

ABBEVILLE PRESS PUBLISHERS NEW YORK LONDON PARIS

JACKET FRONT: The palm-lined entrance to Retiro.
JACKET BACK: A traditionally furnished parlor at Bonsucesso
(see also page 95).
PAGE 1: Detail of the façade at Santa Clara.
FRONTISPIECE: Detail of the kitchen at Secretário
(see also page 46).
PAGES 4–5: The great house and garden at São Fernando
(see also pages 82–83).
PAGE 6: The veranda at Ubá
(see also page 75).

EDITOR: Jacqueline Decter
DESIGNER: Molly Shields
PRODUCTION EDITOR: Abigail Asher
PRODUCTION MANAGER: Lou Bilka
HISTORICAL RESEARCH: Herculano Gomes Mathias
MAP: Sophie Kittredge

First edition
10 9 8 7 6 5 4 3 2 1

Library of Congress Cataloging-in-Publication Data
Pires, Fernando Tasso Fragoso.
    Fazendas : The great houses and plantations of Brazil /
Fernando Tasso Fragoso Pires ; photographs by Nicolas
Sapieha ; translated from the Portuguese by Gregory Rabassa.
        p.   cm.
Includes bibliographical references and index.
ISBN 1-55859-876-6
    1. Plantations—Brazil. 2. Architecture, Colonial—Brazil.
I. Sapieha, Nicolas. II. Title.
NA7298.P57 1995
728.8′0981—dc20   95-24443

I dedicate this book to my wife, Anna Lúcia, and my children, Angela, Monica, Beatriz, Laura, Cristiana, and Pedro. They are the joy of my life.

ACKNOWLEDGMENTS

I would like to thank the following people, all of whom helped make this book possible: Arthur Mário Vianna, Carlos Alberto Adão, Rafael Fragoso Pires, Roberto Menezes de Moraes, and Eduardo Pessôa de Queiroz.
—Fernando Tasso Fragoso Pires

CONTENTS

INTRODUCTION

Under the lens of history, Brazil's rural houses reflect the country's major economic cycles. They evince the predominance of agriculture and cattle herding, and their interior decor bears witness to a thriving social and cultural life. Until the end of the Second Empire in 1889, rural society was of a patriarchal and slave-holding nature, and the element that perhaps best illustrates the system is the *casa-grande*, or great house, the residence of the "master," the center around which everything revolved.

In Brazil, rural property generally finds its name preceded by the term *fazenda*. Old sugar plantations would have *engenho* (mill) in front of their names. Engenho could mean the great house itself as well as the whole sugar-producing complex: mill, warehouses, slave quarters, cane fields, pastures, forest preserves. Today's plantations are called *usinas*. Those still called engenhos are most often plantations that furnish cane for the larger usinas. In the southernmost state of Rio Grande do Sul the great cattle fazendas are called *estâncias*, a Spanish influence.

The subject of this book is Brazil's sugar and coffee plantations and, in the south, its cattle ranches. The opulent mansions that appeared as a consequence of the gold cycle lie outside its scope, for they are located in urban areas. Also excluded are houses connected with economic cycles of lesser impact, notably those of rubber in Amazonas and Pará and cacao in Bahia.

THE SUGAR PLANTATION

The engenho preceded the fazenda and the estância. The first cane fields and mills appeared shortly after the discovery of Brazil by the Portuguese in 1500, and years before the Crown officially occupied the coast of the colony in 1535. Their administrative system divided the colony into hereditary "captaincies"—the nuclei of the future provinces of the Empire (1822–89) and the states of the Republic (1890 on). Along with dyewood, sugar cane was the principal attraction.

Of all the captaincies, Pernambuco was the most successful. Its grantee, Duarte Coelho, established a dialogue with the natives and skillfully organized the political and administrative life of his domains. In a few years he was exporting not only sugar but tobacco and cotton to the homeland and the other captaincies. At his death in 1554, Duarte left a prosperous region to his children, along with the knowledge that the land itself—then as now—belonged to the Indians.

Bahia was the other important sugar-producing region. The early days of its captaincy, however, differed considerably from those of Pernambuco. Named grantee in 1536, Francisco Pereira Coutinho proved to be a poor administrator and was responsible for the failure of colonization during the pioneering phase. For some years Bahia had been settled by Portuguese, Spaniards, and Indians, all of whom lived in harmony under the leadership of Diogo Alvares, the legendary "Caramuru" of Brazilian history. Under official pressure and with the help of Diogo, the region came to know relative progress, with cane fields and sugar mills stretching along the shores of Rencôncavo Bay.

The peaceful coexistence among colonists and natives was shattered, however, by abuses on the part of Coutinho's underlings and the colonists in general when they were not restrained by the authorities. In spite of the intervention of Caramuru and his Indian wife and father-in-law, the conflicts between natives and colonists erupted into a general revolt against the Portuguese, resulting in wholesale destruction. The grantee was forced to flee to the neighboring captaincy of Porto Seguro. When he later attempted to return to Bahia, he was captured and killed by the natives.

The fighting in Bahia brought on a decline in sugar production, and it went against the plans of the Portuguese Crown. Moreover, French ships were prowling along the coast, planning an invasion of the land "in order to rebuild the plantations and sugar mills," as the grantee of Porto Seguro reported in a letter to the king of Portugal. Taking this information into account and keeping in mind the special conditions of the Recôncavo for the cultivation of sugar cane, King John III took back the captaincy for the Crown and decided to set up a general government in Bahia through which the colony could be better ruled. When the arrangement was formalized, Tomé de Souza was named governor general. His first act after taking office in 1549 was to transfer the village of Vila Velha to a higher and more protected location, where he founded São Salvador da Bahia de Todos os Santos, or, simply, Salvador, the capital of Brazil until 1763.

Although the reestablishment of sugar production was his principal concern, the governor general also sought to unify colonial administration, repress grantees' excesses, prevent abuses against natives, regulate relations between captaincies, solidify coastal defenses, and organize the colony judicially and politically. With all these measures, an irreversible process of colonization was set in motion, a move powerfully reinforced by the arrival of Jesuit priests.

During this period, the first African slaves were brought into the colony. The colonists needed laborers capable of sustaining and increasing the cultivation of cane, and they did not think the Indians would ever submit to a system of slavery. With the introduction of slave labor, a fundamental distinction arose between Portugal and Brazil. While in the mother country the scarcity of land led to the adoption of a wage system, in the colony, where land was abundant and could be exploited to fulfill the demands of the European economy, the adoption of slavery assured the survival of the colonial economy.

The sugar cycle became firmly established during the governorship of Mem de Sá (1558–72), with land grants to those prepared to invest in the activity. By 1570 the colony had almost a hundred plantations, and sugar accounted for nearly three-quarters of its exports. The cycle reached its peak in the final decades of the sixteenth century and continued to prosper until the Dutch invasions. A combination of factors was responsible for its growth: the high price of the product on the European market; increased consumption, precisely because of the introduction of Brazilian sugar; and a commercial monopoly in the hands of the mother country, which put constant pressure on the producing captaincies. The government and the plantation owners were partners in the enterprise: the former awarded land and financing; the latter lent military aid, which they were legally obliged to do.

Although none of the plantations of those days have survived, the narratives of Gabriel Soares and Fernão Cardim, who traveled through Pernambuco and Bahia in 1584, chronicle the luxury of the houses, the income of the owners, the plethora of gold and silver items, the jewelry and silks of the women, the velvets and damasks of the men, the fine furniture, and the large number of slaves. Soares states: "One finds more vanity in Pernambuco than in Lisbon." And Cardim, facing a loaded table and many guests, observes: "They have the appearance of counts and do a lot of spending."

In every prosperous society the stage that leads it to excess is generally a forewarning of its decline. In the 1620s the four-hundred-year sugar cycle reached that stage, catalyzed by the devastation of the forests surrounding the coastal plantations, which left firewood in short supply and necessitated the relocation of the mills farther inland at great expense. Another factor was a series of political events in Europe that would culminate in the Dutch invasions.

For dynastic reasons, the thrones of Portugal and Spain were united in 1581, and the sugar trade was gradually taken over by the Spanish. Interested in protecting the sugar produced on Madeira from competition, King Philip II sought to close Iberian ports to Dutch commerce, imposing an economic embargo that made access to Brazilian sugar difficult. Professor Celso Furtado summarizes the reasons for the Dutch invasions of Brazil: "At the beginning of the seventeenth century the Dutch controlled practically all maritime commerce in Europe. Distributing sugar in Europe without the cooperation of Dutch merchants was obviously impractical. In addition, the Dutch were not at all prepared to give up the substantial role they played in that important business, the success of which had been to a large degree due to their work. The struggle for the control of sugar became, in this way, one of the basic reasons for the all-out war that the Dutch waged against Spain, and one of the episodes in that war was the occupation by Holland of a large part of the sugar-producing region of Brazil for a quarter of a century."

The Dutch invaded Bahia between 1624 and 1625 without much success. Their invasion of Pernambuco was more successful and lasted much longer, from 1630 to 1654. The period of the Dutch occupation—and the presence in Brazil of Prince Maurice of Nassau Siegen, Administrator of Dutch Brazil—is one of the most interesting chapters in the history of the Portuguese colony. For the seventeenth-century sugar economy, however, it was devastating. Attacked by land and sea in long and countless clashes, the captaincies saw their cities and towns occupied, their cane fields destroyed, their sugar mills burned, and their stores of sugar captured. They suffered the flight of plantation workers, a lack of transport, a loss of harvests. In the meantime, many of the Dutch took the expertise they acquired on Pernambucan plantations and moved to their Caribbean possessions, where they set up production, motivated by the high price sugar was commanding as a result of dwindling Brazilian reserves. This combination of events kept Brazil's economy in crisis for many years. The participation of Brazilian sugar on the market decreased from 80 percent in 1630 to 10 percent in 1700.

At the turn of the eighteenth century wars in Europe caused an encouraging rise in sugar prices, just when Pernambuco and Bahia were attempting to revive production. The prospects of recuperation would prove illusory, however, owing to the discovery of gold and diamonds in what is now the state of Minas Gerais. The Portuguese Crown, disheartened by the instability of the sugar trade and dazzled by the new riches, turned its attention from sugar to gold, thus initiating a new economic cycle in Brazil. The settlement of Brazil's interior territory owes much to the ambitious search for the precious metal. As the population of the south-central region of Brazil grew, the south came to dominate the north, the capital moved from Salvador to Rio de Janeiro, and the fortunes of São Paulo began to rise.

Sugar production experienced difficulties throughout the eighteenth century. The price of slaves was inflated by the gold mines, which paid better. Oxen and horses, indispensable to both enterprises, also became more expensive as demand increased. The mines received preferential treatment in obtaining basic supplies because they paid in gold instead of sugar. Finally, however, toward the end of the century the situation underwent a radical transformation. With gold reserves dwindling, miners began returning to agriculture. And with France and England at war (1793), shipping to America was interrupted, hurting the Antillean economy but benefiting Brazil.

The flatlands north of Rio de Janeiro abandoned cattle, the main activity until then, and became a splendid new center of sugar production. It wasn't long before the city of Rio de Janeiro had sugar plantations all around it. The plantation owners of the region enjoyed great status, as the learned French traveler and botanist Augustin François César Provençal de Saint-Hilaire reported in one of his chronicles: "The ownership of a sugar plantation confers, among Rio de Janeiro agriculturalists, a kind of nobility. One speaks only with great respect of a plantation owner and acquiring such preeminence is the general ambition."

At the dawn of the nineteenth century the sugar centers of the colony experienced a phase of optimism and hope. It was to be the second, and last, peak of the cycle. Among the factors contributing to it were political disturbances in the Caribbean, the Continental Blockade in Europe, and the consequent downturn in the economy of Central America and the Caribbean. These events provided an opportunity for an expansion of Brazilian sugar production.

Pressed by the need to increase production, plantation owners began to introduce new equipment and techniques: iron grinders replaced age-old wooden rollers; plows replaced hoes; and steam engines replaced water power. Steamships with greater capacity made transportation cheaper. In some cases the modernizations prompted the merger of two or more plantations to increase manpower and, especially, capital. Out of these unions arose even more powerful plantation owners.

Sugar wealth attracted titles of nobility, and a new, aristocratized agrarian society reigned over the sugar regions, a society no longer rustic or reclusive, but sophisticated and interested in cultural development and in providing a better education for family members. New manor houses were built or old ones enlarged.

The interiors were enriched, the gardens beautified. Coats of arms adorned walls, ceilings, decorative objects, and tableware. Plantations situated by the water installed fish hatcheries both for sport and for provisions. Vast fields of sugar cane and the natural tropical beauty of the land framed the seat of each establishment.

But this euphoric period did not last beyond the middle of the nineteenth century, when the sumptuous sugar civilization went into a decline from which it never recovered. The problems were insurmountable: growing competition from the Antillean colonies, which were flooding the market with sugar of superior quality; the discovery of beet sugar, which made former consumers of Brazilian sugar self-sufficient; and the cultivation of coffee in the province of Rio de Janeiro. If in the eighteenth century gold had been responsible for crushing sugar interests, in the nineteenth the culprit was the coffee trade, a new phenomenon that burst forth about the time independence was proclaimed (1822).

Most of the sugar-plantation houses that survive have long been abandoned and lie in ruins. Thanks to a new awareness of preservation, some are slowly being restored with private funds. Little is known about the architectural influences on these early houses. The primary source of information are descriptions by chroniclers of the period, notably those of the aforementioned Soares and Cardim. The owners' legal obligations to construct watchtowers on their houses as a means of defense suggests fortresslike structures, and seventeenth-century illustrations confirm this.

Although there are no extant sixteenth-century plantations, a few of their chapels have survived, and over time have passed from private to public ownership. In the Gávea district of Rio de Janeiro, for example, the church of Our Lady of the Conception was originally the chapel of the sixteenth-century plantation by the same name. Within the bounds of the Freguesia plantation, on the island of Maré in the Bay of Bahia, the chapel of Our Lady of the Snows resists time, having been built in the middle of the century of discovery on the plantation of André Margalho.

During the Dutch occupation, the Dutch artists Franz Post and Albert Eckhout lived in Brazil. Paintings from Post's series "Brazilian Landscapes" provide a visual record of the different kinds of plantations of that time. The more affluent featured a two-story great house with a watchtower, a chapel, and a mill. The more modest lacked a separate chapel; the houses, of lath-and-plaster construction, also consisted of two stories, but had no towers.

The most opulent sugar-plantation houses date from the eighteenth century. Clearly influenced by Portuguese baroque architecture, these palatial residences were usually square or rectangular in shape, with thick walls of stone and mortar. They often featured an inner courtyard. Three, sometimes even four, stories high, their interiors were richly decorated. Chapels, whether attached to the houses or separate from them, resembled churches, their walls often covered with framed paintings. The Freguesia plantation in Bahia, now a museum, preserves the memory of these monumental eighteenth-century plantation houses (see pages 184–89).

An "intermediate" type of eighteenth-century sugar-plantation house was rectangular in shape but had no inner courtyard. Public and family rooms occupied the second floor; service areas and lodgings were relegated to the first. The more elegant houses of this type boasted an attic.

About the turn of the nineteenth century, the classic type of plantation house emerged. A low, one-story dwelling with a basement that served only as ventilation, it typically featured a veranda running the length of the front façade. Based on an urban for the great house, which dominated all the other buildings. Often royal palms lined the road leading to the house and enhanced its garden. Ponds, springs, fountains, and statues completed the external decoration of the residence.

No expense was spared on sculpted stone to decorate doors, windows, balconies, and staircases. The indispensable tanks and sluiceways for the water that kept the coffee beans moving were made out of the same stone. They were true masterpieces of the stonecutter's art. Most large plantations also featured a walled orchard and a wrought-iron entrance gate.

No plantation was complete without a chapel, whether a separate structure or part of the house. The interiors of the houses were decorated with refinement. Everything was imported from Europe: the wallpaper, the Sèvres porcelain emblazoned with coats of arms, the silver vessels, the tapestries, the drapery, the crystal, and the furnishings, as well as the plasterers, stonecutters, and painters.

Oil painting of the fazenda Retiro (see pages 48–55) by Johann Georg Grimm, 1881, showing the typical square-shaped configuration of coffee plantations. The terreiro *is surrounded by outbuildings on three sides, with the great house occupying the fourth.*

Two-story houses had elegant carved-wood staircases. It was customary for oil portraits of the owners and members of their families to hang in galleries alongside portraits of their imperial majesties.

In addition to plantation houses, the wealthier coffee barons built mansions in the cities of the Paraíba valley—including Piraí, Valença, Paraíba do Sul, and especially Vassouras—and even in the capital, where they would send their children to study or to board the "steamer" for European sojourns. Throughout the prosperous years of the coffee cycle the population grew, and cities and towns burgeoned, becoming the heart of a new civilization, sophisticated in its customs and manners. French was spoken, literature was cultivated, and music and lyric theater were enjoyed. The chroniclers of the period record memorable functions, both on the plantations and in the urban residences, at which the owners played host to visitors from the capital, and young ladies and gentlemen from the plantations had the opportunity to come together. Under parental supervision marriages were arranged, usually for the merging of lands. The emperor himself was often received on plantations or in the towns with great fanfare. There was no lack of philanthropy on the part of coffee growers, who helped fund the building of churches, bridges, viaducts, fountains, and hospitals. Thus the coffee cycle produced a real revolution in the customs of the province.

Nowhere was this cultural advancement felt more tangibly than in Vassouras: the beautiful square shaded by palm trees, with a large granite fountain at its center, graceful church on its high point, and barons' mansions all around; daily newspapers; good schools; and bustling traffic. Jewelers, watchmakers, and French fashion designers all lent a cosmopolitan air to the young town, which attained the category of city in 1857. And to think that a little red berry was solely responsible for this extraordinary growth! In 1848, at a ball in honor of Emperor Pedro II, who was on an official visit to the town, the ladies paid homage to the source of their good fortune by decorating their coiffures with coffee sprigs.

A coffee grower's wealth was calculated by the amount of land and the number of slaves he owned. Those who owned a hundred *alqueires* (an *alqueire* is equivalent to about twelve acres) and fifty slaves were considered small growers. Larger ones owned between three and six hundred *alqueires*, comprising one or more plantations, and no fewer than two hundred slaves. The wealthiest of all were the owners of latifundias, large estates with eight hundred, a thousand, or even more *alqueires*, and thousands of slaves.

The Rio de Janeiro coffee cycle reached its height in the 1850s. The harvest of 1855 was the greatest of all, but it also marked the dividing line between the cycle's rise and fall. One of the first obstacles the coffee barons encountered was a decrease in labor resulting from the 1850 law prohibiting the African slave trade. The situation was eased somewhat by the purchase of slaves from the declining sugar plantations and gold mines. Their labor was essential to Brazil's development. As historian Alberto Lamego writes, "Despite the stigma of a brutal slavery-based feudalism . . . no other system could have carried out the colossal and complete change in the environment of the mountains. Only the savagery of slave labor succeeded in removing the virgin forest, preparing it for a future industrial evolution by means of an initial stage that was exclusively agrarian."

Another problem that beset the coffee growers was an outbreak of coffee-tree diseases that reached epidemic proportions. The groves in the virgin lands of the Paraíba valley were not affected at first, but eventually they would be plagued by periodic infestations. For a while production continued to increase nonetheless, because more and more plantations were being established; by 1860, however, productivity was no longer the same.

Still another factor contributing to the decline of the cycle was the practice of clear-cutting, which caused a change in climatic conditions. Moreover, the complete ignorance of ecologically sound planting techniques resulted in the erosion of the fertile topsoil. To compensate for the depletion of the soil and the drop in its productivity, more land, more labor, and more investment were required, and many of the producers soon found themselves deep in debt. By 1880 the Rio coffee economy was faced with disintegration.

Abolitionist propaganda increased, gaining the sympathy of the emperor himself. In tense meetings plantation owners strove to find solutions. Attempted without success was the immigration of unskilled Chinese workers as a substitute for Africans, who were on the eve of their yearned-for freedom. European immigrants found no attraction in the province of Rio, with its depleted land and dearth of available capital. They preferred the red earth of São Paulo, where the planting of coffee by free workers would take hold under the Republic, establishing a stable and realistic agricultural economy.

"Slavery is over in Brazil. Laws to the contrary are revoked." With that simple pronouncement, the law abolishing slavery was laid down by the Princess Regent in May 1888, on the eve of the harvest. Unpicked, the berries rotted among the growing weeds of the abandoned fields. With their plantations mortgaged and no means to redeem them, the impoverished owners and their families confronted the difficult transition to a new reality.

The fall of the monarchy in 1889, one year after abolition, swept away the remains of Rio's rural aristocracy. Beginning in 1890, the high price of coffee on the international market went toward enriching the growers in São Paulo, and coffee would continue to be Brazil's main export through the first half of the twentieth century.

The coffee culture of the province of Rio de Janeiro had much in common with the roughly contemporaneous cotton culture of the American state of Georgia,

The great house at São Martinho da Esperança,
as it looked before it was remodeled in the 1940s
(see pages 132–39).

the story of which was immortalized in Margaret Mitchell's novel *Gone with the Wind*. Both cultures developed a strict social hierarchy ruled by an opulent agrarian aristocracy whose luxurious way of life was supported by a slave-holding system. Both Rio coffee and Georgia cotton left architectural evidence attesting to the grandeur of their respective cultures. The surviving plantation houses of the American South recall the fictional Tara of *Gone with the Wind*, while the great houses of such fazendas as Paraíso and Secretário, both featured in this book, are tangible reminders of the coffee cycle's heyday.

Even the beautiful, rich, impetuous character of Scarlett O'Hara has her parallel in the *sinhàzinha*, or daughter of the great house. Perhaps the most renowned *sinhàzinha* was Euphrasia Teixeira Leite. The daughter and granddaughter of coffee barons, she was prevented by her family from marrying her great love, the famous anti-slavery diplomat Joaquim Nabuco. In rebellion, she moved to Paris, where her elegant mansion at 40, rue du Bassano near the Eiffel Tower became a gathering place for artists and intellectuals. With her lavish life-style supported by coffee money, Euphrasia became known simply as "The Brazilian." Years later, still willful, capricious, and single, she returned to her native Vassouras, to which she left her whole fortune, today evident in schools and hospitals. Her legacy is preserved in a museum called House of the Era, the mansion where she had been born and raised.

Finally, the greatest similarity between the two agrarian cultures was their ephemeral nature. The masters of both shared the firm belief that their good fortune would last forever. They failed to notice the end approaching until it was too late, and their societies were already becoming part of history.

THE CATTLE RANCH

The last part of Brazil to be settled was the territory comprising the present-day state of Rio Grande do Sul. The 1494 Treaty of Tordesillas was the major obstacle against the immediate occupation of the land. Dividing Portuguese and Spanish sovereignty over their New World discoveries, the treaty's line of demarcation passed right through the area, causing friction between the two nations and hesitation on both their parts to colonize the region throughout the sixteenth and seventeenth centuries.

During this period of uncertain frontiers, Spanish Jesuit missionaries moved into the area from Paraguay. It was the Spanish Crown's idea that religion might be the most effective means of pacifying the Indians and winning them over as allies in the conquest of new lands and the exploitation of their riches. The Jesuits introduced both education and cattle ranches into the disputed territory.

The missionaries' interest in cattle raising was to provide the Indians with food so that they would remain in their settlements instead of moving from place to place to hunt and fish. In this way the Jesuits succeeded in establishing missionary centers.

To insure the rapid growth of herds, the missionaries decided to limit slaughter. That decision, along with the good pastureland, allowed the cattle to multiply with extraordinary speed.

Throughout the seventeenth century groups of *bandeirantes*, or trailblazers, from São Paulo headed south in an attempt to find Indians for capture and enslavement. They also had their eyes on the land. The missionaries put up a fierce fight against these invaders but were frequently forced to relocate their missions. Between 1636 and 1640 many missionary villages were wiped out and the inhabitants killed. The survivors fled with the Jesuits, crossing the Uruguay River.

For decades thereafter cattle roamed the plains, breeding in complete freedom. But in 1680 Portugal took the first step toward consolidating what it considered its southern domains by establishing the colony of Sacramento, administered directly by the viceroy in Rio de Janeiro. This was followed in 1682 by the setting up of a base in Laguna on the Santa Catarina shore. Intermediate ports in Paranaguá, São Francisco, and Ilha do Desterro (Florianópolis today) helped to control the vast territory.

When the trailblazing came to an end in the last years of the seventeenth century, the Jesuits returned with their converts to the left bank of the Uruguay, drawn by the large number of herds that grazed there. Thus began the Jesuits' second penetration into the area; it would last until their expulsion from Brazil in the mid-eighteenth century. If the first penetration was prompted by a desire to educate and convert the Indians, the second was fueled by hostility toward Spanish rule. A new national feeling was taking shape, and the first tangible expression of it was the founding of the Seven Missionary Villages, a story that still captures the imagination of artists and writers. These legendary missions were the nuclei of future cities, the embryos of Rio Grande do Sul civilization, and the points of origin for the spread of its cultural values.

After the Jesuits were expelled, the fields were abandoned once more, and the cattle were at the mercy of anyone who wished to capture them. The missionaries' breeding ranches were taken over by colonizers, already the beneficiaries of land grants, which were awarded to those who helped in military actions brought on by disputes over the ownership of the territory.

Fundamental to the development of the region was the road to Sorocaba. Opened in 1727, it crossed the plains of Curitiba until it reached the city of Sorocaba, the great cattle-trading emporium in São Paulo province. The road would make Rio Grande do Sul the primary source of meat, horses, and mules for the gold and diamond mines in Minas Gerais. And when the gold petered out, the region would provide dried beef to the coffee growers in the Paraíba valley. Thus, in an indirect way Brazil's other economic cycles—sugar, gold, and coffee—contributed to the south's integration into the rest of the country.

The end of the eighteenth century also brought an end to the period of predatory land conquest. The invaders from central Brazil turned toward other interests, and in 1801 the border dispute between Spain and Portugal was finally resolved, with the territory becoming Portuguese. By 1807, when the dependent

The aristocratic life of Santo Antônio (see pages 148–53) in 1920: from left to right, Olívia Guedes Penteado, her daughter Carolina Penteado da Silva Telles (present owner of the plantation along with her five children), and a niece, in a charrette, also known as a "little basket," brought from Paris.

captaincy of São Pedro (Rio Grande do Sul) was founded, the region had already taken on a distinct profile. Estâncias, or ranches, had begun producing salted meat, and wealthy cattle dealers acquired a status and social position that put them in the upper echelons of society. The number of estâncias expanded rapidly under generously awarded land grants. At the time of independence in 1822, cattle numbered more than five million head. The region of the present-day city of Pelotas developed a prosperous network of meat-drying facilities and leather-processing plants. Cattle raising was originally centered in the region known as Campanha, with its main grazing lands near the southern border of the future state of Rio Grande do Sul.

The first president of the province, the Viscount of São Leopoldo, was responsible for creating a colony of Germans in Rio Grande do Sul. The first group of Germans landed in Porto Alegre in 1824. Dedicating themselves to farming in the valley of the Sinos River, they fulfilled the needs of the great cattle ranches, assuring them an indispensable subsistence base. That wave of immigration went on for forty years. After 1870 the flow of Europeans was reinforced by Italians, who cultivated grapes and established vineyards. The flourishing farms of the European immigrants also contributed to the feeding of troops during the armed conflicts that faced the independent Brazilian nation.

The Bank of the Province, founded in 1858, became an important factor in the wealth of Rio Grande do Sul, underwriting the development of its leather industry and the building of railroads in the second half of the nineteenth century. But by the time the Republic was proclaimed in 1890, the province's economy was in recession because of a drop in the consumption of dried beef. Gradually, however, the establishments that produced dried beef were modernized, and a major meat industry, catering primarily to foreign markets, developed.

The ranches in the northern part of Rio Grande do Sul received the generic designation *fazendas*, while those closer to the border with Uruguay and Argentina are called *estâncias*. The houses built on the latter, usually inspired by Spanish colonial architecture, were at first designed to meet the necessities of defense; many featured high walls for better protection. They tended to have an austere simplicity, and although some were quite large, they offered no great comfort or luxury. Elegant, imported furnishings were rare. Gardens were characteristically absent on these ranches. Pastureland literally came right up to the walls of the house. As a rule, the houses on the southern ranches did not aspire to the same level of grandeur or sophistication as those of the sugar and coffee plantations.

PAU GRANDE

Unlike most coffee fazendas, Pau Grande (Big Tree) existed long before the coffee cycle began. Originally a sugar plantation, its founding toward the end of the seventeenth century coincided with the opening of the most important highway in colonial Brazil, the legendary "New Road to Minas Gerais," built by Garcia Rodrigues Paes and Pedro de Morais Raposo. According to family tradition, a huge jacaranda tree that had been felled by lightning marked the exact point of entry onto the plantation.

Multicolored bougainvillea in full bloom grace the rear garden at Pau Grande. The windowed tower is the cupola of the chapel.

The first owner was the Viscount of Asseca, Martim Correa de Sá, a member of the largest landowning family in Rio de Janeiro for two centuries. As of 1748, however, the land had passed to the Gomes Ribeiro family, which would own Pau Grande right up to the twentieth century. At the end of the eighteenth century, seventeen land grants, including Ubá, Guaribu, and Pau Grande, were grouped together, and José Rodrigues da Cruz, Antônio Ribeiro de Avelar, José Rodrigues Pereira de Almeida, and Antônio dos Santos formed a corporation named House of Pau Grande. That organization built a huge sugar mill on the plantation, the second-largest privately owned one in Brazil at the time. Pau Grande grew, raised, and manufactured everything it needed: grain, sugar, donkeys, horses, and tools.

The location of the fazenda on the New Road made it a stopping point for travelers, including French naturalist Auguste Saint-Hilaire and José Joaquim da Silva Xavier, known as Tiradentes, who instigated the first rebellion against Portuguese rule in 1789. Tiradentes was hanged for his

ABOVE: *A former bedroom has been transformed into a modern bathroom. The bathtub was carved out of a single piece of marble, a common practice in the nineteenth century.*

OPPOSITE: *A reception room on the ground floor is furnished with twentieth-century Brazilian pieces.*

insurrection by order of Queen Maria I of Portugal. Antônio Ribeiro de Avelar's involvement with the revolutionary hero put him under tremendous political pressure, cost him an enormous sum to avoid the "inquiry," and precipitated his death in 1794. The hostile climate obliged the family to retire to the plantation, and in 1797 Luís Gomes Ribeiro, Antônio's son-in-law and heir, assumed control of the business along with Antônio's widow. José Rodrigues da Cruz withdrew to found the neighboring plantation of Ubá, which, according to Saint-Hilaire, was inhabited "by wild Indians" (see pages 68–75).

Luís Ribeiro began construction of the great house that today surprises and charms tourists with its architectural grandeur and physical beauty. Dating from the first decade of the nineteenth century, it consists of two distinct wings separated by a chapel. Luís and his mother-in-law wisely lived in separate wings. The eighteen wrought-iron balconies gracing the upper-story windows of the house were imported from Lisbon. Those balconies, a luxury for their time, impressed Saint-Hilaire, who said of the house, "Pau Grande reminds one less of our castles than of a monastery."

Luís Ribeiro remained on the plantation until 1810, when disagreements with his mother-in-law led him to withdraw to the Guaribu plantation, where he would live until his death in 1839. His brother-in-law Joaquim Ribeiro de Avelar, the future Baron of Capivari, became master of Pau Grande during the golden age of coffee. Neither Capivari nor any of his brothers or sisters ever married, but the baron recognized an illegitimate son, gave him his name, educated him, and made him his only heir and successor. The second Joaquim Ribeiro de Avelar later received the title Viscount of Ubá. His wife, Mariana, daughter of José Maria Velho da Silva, the major-domo of the Imperial Palace, introduced all the refinements and comforts typical of wealthy homes of the period, including indoor bathrooms. Under her supervision, the mansion filled with furniture, paintings, rugs, porcelain, draperies, and a famed collection of silver objects.

With the death of the Viscount of Ubá in 1888 and the financial difficulties that accompanied the end of the coffee cycle, Pau Grande's decline was inevitable. In the 1930s the writer José Lins do Rego bore witness to its

impoverishment in *Days Come and Gone:* "An old woman in black appeared at the top of the stairs. She was an Avelar and she was telling it all: 'We don't live here. Everything here is finished . . .' and she went along showing us the huge salons, the bedrooms, the furniture in a state of neglect . . . oil paintings could be seen on the walls. The Baron of Capivari in different poses, with the face of a leader, the baron's sisters, three ladies like figures out of an English novel . . . the library. Some two thousand volumes in iron bookcases: La Fontaine, Molière, Victor Hugo, George Sand, the *Revue des deux mondes* . . . the chapel—the tombs were there. . . . The old woman in black spoke: 'Everything was sold to Rio. . . . All this is quite sad.' . . . Suddenly I got the picture," José Lins do Rego concludes, "of that plantation during its days of glory. The baron standing on the balcony looking at the coffee groves as they turned red, the slaves scattered among the trees, the happy family, that great Brazilian happiness. The old woman brought me back to reality, however.

OPPOSITE: The altar and balconies of the two-story chapel are located behind a carved-wood balustrade. Generations of owners and their families are buried beneath the ground floor.

RIGHT: The entrance to the chapel is on the ground floor underneath the choir loft.

OPPOSITE: *The great house is a harmonious blend of traditional Luso-Brazilian and neo-classical architecture. According to professor of architecture Key Imaguire, "a markedly colonial element is the double row of panes topped by a segmental arch above each of the full-length casement windows. Neoclassical in style are the three staircases leading up to the house." On the right is the former sugar mill, now a stable.*

BELOW: *The left wing of the house overlooks a garden and the pool. The unadorned second-story sash windows are reminiscent of those in eighteenth-century monasteries or convents.*

She wanted to be nice to us. And in chipped cups without handles she served us demitasse. It was all she had to offer."

After the Ribeiro de Avelars, and with its area reduced to less than 250 acres, the fazenda came into the possession of art collector Plácido Gutiérrez and then went to businesswoman Lily de Carvalho Marinho. In the 1980s businessman Walter Soares Ribas acquired it, undertook its restoration, and furnished the house with Brazilian pieces from various periods. Every two bedrooms—out of a total of twenty-six—were converted into a suite with a bedroom and bath. In this way he succeeded in modernizing the house without knocking down any walls.

The roof of the old sugar mill now shelters a stable for the long-maned pacers bred there, the main activity on the fazenda, and a modern barn for dairy cows has been built. Pau Grande's imposing stone masonry

is outstanding, especially the rounded foundations of the various outbuildings. Also noteworthy are the cold-storage building (where meat was kept before the advent of refrigeration) and the three staircases leading to the garden at the front of the house—all works of art in stone. Located ten miles from the town of Avelar on a paved road, Pau Grande, renewed and revived, is one of the most extraordinary rural houses in Brazil.

PARAÍSO

The two iron statues flanking the main staircase stand vigil over the spot where the Viscount of Rio Preto, master of Paraíso, met his death in 1868.

H istorian Carlos Alberto d'Araújo Guimarães called Paraíso "the jewel of Valença," and the description holds true to this day. "In its simple grandeur the house possesses the serenity of a city mansion," he writes in his book *The Court in Brazil.* "Resplendent in their luxury are the style of the furniture, the purity of the crystal and the mirrors, the designs of the fine tapestries, the sobriety of the damasks, and the silverwork. Galleries of valuable paintings, a museum of treasures, a chapel— the fazenda has it all." Indeed, even though more than a century has passed since the height of the coffee cycle, the great house at Paraíso is still one of the most extraordinary examples of Brazilian rural architecture. If a vague memory is alive in its soul, reality is felt in its body of stone and mortar.

Unlike so many plantation houses, which were one-story structures over a storage basement, the great house at Paraíso is a two-story residence, with one whole side occupied by the chapel and choir loft and the other by service areas. The main body of the house has public rooms on the first floor and private rooms on the second. A drive flanked by royal palms leads from the road to the iron entrance gate of the garden. Professor of Brazilian architecture Key Imaguire Júnior finds elements of both eighteenth-century colonial and nineteenth-century neoclassical architecture in the house's exterior and interior structures. The segmental arch over the main door is an example of the former and the steps and columns of the vestibule are typical of the latter. Also tending toward the colonial are the wide floor boards, the so-called "skirt-and-blouse" ceiling treatment, and the roofing tiles. However, the house is less a syncretism of the colonial and neoclassical styles than an

ABOVE: *One of several trompe l'oeil wall paintings in the dining room featuring culinary themes.*

LEFT: *The large mural in the main dining room depicts Rio de Janeiro's Guanabara Bay in 1860 with Corcovado and Sugar Loaf mountains in the background. All of the murals and trompe l'oeil paintings in the fazenda are the work of Catalan artist José Maria Villaronga.*

eclectic combination of the two for maximum ornamental effect, as seen in the walls painted to imitate marble, the decoratively patterned wallpaper, and the parquet floors of the interior, as well as in the stonework of the exterior.

Located near the Manuel Duarte district, five miles from the town of Rio das Flores, the Flores do Paraíso plantation—its original name—has its roots in the grants awarded by the Portuguese government to Manuel Jacinto Nogueira da Gama, the future Marquis of Baependi. Bordered on the south by the Paraíba do Sul River and on the north by the Preto River, this area was at the turn of the nineteenth century taken by force from the Indians, who unsuccessfully tried to impede the penetration of the white invaders.

The first owner of the plantation, João Pedro Maynard d'Afonseca e Sá, began clearing the forest and farming the land in 1810. A year after his death in 1836, his widow and heiress, Joana Ediviges de Menezes e Souza sold the property to Domingos Custódio Guimarães, the future Viscount of Rio Preto, who became the great plantation master of Paraíso for thirty years.

OPPOSITE: A trompe l'oeil trellis and classical sculpture decorate the walls of the main stairwell.

BELOW: Detail of the Villaronga mural in the dining room.

The construction of the magnificent house was completed in 1845. The wealthy viscount did not spare any expense to endow the interior "with every comfort that European industry and genius could produce," according to Araújo Guimarães.

The Viscount of Rio Preto enlarged his domains, founding or acquiring ten other important coffee plantations, including Loanda, São Policarpo, Santa Genoveva, Santa Rosa, Monte Alverne, and Santa Luzia. He was one of the most representative figures of rural aristocracy in the province of Rio de Janeiro. One of his most notable charitable works for Rio Preto was the founding of the Holy House of Mercy in Valença, a city of which he was a benefactor and where he had a mansion that still stands.

With the opening of the Union and Industry Highway linking Petrópolis in the province of Rio to Juiz de Fora in Minas Gerais, Domingos Custódio urged its builder, Mariano Procópio Ferreira Lage, to construct

ABOVE: *Exuberant in its eclectic adaptation of architectural styles, Paraíso is truly "the jewel of Valença." All the outbuildings erected during its coffee-producing days still surround it.*

OPPOSITE: *The carved stonework above the ground-floor windows, and elsewhere, serves a purely ornamental function.*

an auxiliary road that would connect the new highway to the town of Porto das Flores on the bank of the Preto River, thereby facilitating the transport of coffee from Valença, which had been virtually isolated from any highway.

The road was built, and its opening celebration was set for September 7, 1868, the viscount's birthday. As the great house at Paraíso filled with prestigious guests from the province and the capital, the Viscount of Rio Preto arrived by carriage from Loanda. Alighting at the entrance, he suffered a sudden massive heart attack, and fell to the ground, dead.

The viscount's widow died five years later, leaving Paraíso to their son Domingos Custódio Guimarães Júnior. Awarded the title Baron of Rio Preto, Domingos Júnior was master of the plantation during another prosperous phase of the coffee cycle but died young, in 1876. Paraíso stayed in the family until 1895, when it was sold to Manuel Vieira Machado da Cunha, Baron of Aliança. In 1912 the Baron of Aliança sold it to Galileu Belfort Arantes and his brother Antônio Belfort Arantes. Buying out Antônio in 1941, Galileu became sole owner. On his death he was succeeded by his daughter and grandchildren, in whose possession the fazenda remains, administered by his grandson Paulo Roberto Belfort Carneiro da Silva.

With an area of 2,400 acres, Paraíso is now in the business of raising beef and dairy cattle. Served by an excellent paved road that passes a few yards from the mansion, the plantation's great house retains its architectural elegance, a serene sight at the end of the palm-tree-lined drive.

CHACRINHA

The tea parlor at Chacrinha is decorated with nineteenth-century Brazilian furniture. The frame of the cane-backed Louis-Philippe armchair in the foreground is of jacaranda, the wood of a native Brazilian tree.

Founded in the 1880s, toward the end of the coffee cycle, Chacrinha's prosperity as a coffee plantation was not destined to last for long. Named for the site chosen for its great house (*chacrinha* is the diminutive of *chácara*, a piece of rural property), the fazenda was an offshoot of Campo Alegre, an important plantation belonging to Manuel Pereira de Sousa Barros, Baron of Vista Alegre. Chacrinha's establishment was the result of a custom common among coffee-growing families: when a son married and started a new family he would receive his own house on a plantation carved out of the main one. Covering an area of 1,000 acres, Chacrinha is located seven miles from the city of Valença.

An old hand-drawn map by Captain Ignácio de Sousa Werneck, a pioneer in the settlement of the area, shows that unlike other areas of Rio province, the Valença region had not been fully exploited during the eighteenth century. Requests for land grants had been made, but occupation began only at the beginning of the nineteenth century. One of those grants went to Captain Manuel Pereira de Sousa Barros, the father of the Baron of Vista Alegre and the founder of Campo Alegre, who lived on the plantation until his death in 1849. But it was his son and namesake who ran Campo Alegre during the golden age of coffee, and he enjoyed a prestigious social and political position both in the province and in the capital. A passionate follower of thoroughbred racing, he raised horses on the plantation to compete in events at the Derby Club, a racing organization of which he was one of the founders.

"Vista Alegre was one of the most prodigal nabobs of the Empire," wrote historian Gastão Penalva in the *Jornal do Brasil* in March 1937. "A solid fortune of vast land holdings, picture-book coffee groves, lush pastureland, all of which later trickled away down the agile and deceitful legs of race horses." Whether because of horses or because of the collapse of the coffee economy, the baron died poor in 1891 and his widow, who survived him by many years, experienced great hardship. Drowning in debt, with the plantations mortgaged to the Bank of Brazil and numerous others, and with no possibility of covering the promissory notes, in 1893 she told the properties, including Chacrinha, to Nicolau, Vito, and Caetano Pentagna. Immediately thereafter the lands were transferred to the Valença firm of Esteves Brothers & Co., which in turn handed them over to the Bank of Brazil in payment of debts. Auctioned off, they were bought by Álvaro Mendes de Oliveira Castro and his brother Horácio, the first of three generations of Oliveira Castros to own the plantations until the 1980s.

At first Chacrinha and the other plantations in the Campo Alegre

OPPOSITE: This end of the second-story veranda overlooks the lush landscape in front of the house. The modern table and chairs are made of Indian cane.

RIGHT: The veranda runs the entire width of the house. The fanlights above the windows are a typical feature of Luso-Brazilian architecture. Modern wicker furniture provides comfortable seating.

ABOVE: *Colonial in style, Chacrinha's great house was modeled after some of Brazil's most prestigious urban mansions. Built during the final phase of Rio's coffee cycle, it affirmed the economic and social position of its owner.*

OPPOSITE: *The spectacular view from the front of the house takes in the garden, with its inviting pool, royal palms, and espatodeas, which bloom year round; the Flores River; and in the distance the pastures, where coffee trees once flourished.*

group persisted in growing coffee. After a while, however, the one-crop culture was replaced by the breeding of purebred Holstein cows; industrialization followed. Acquired by Pedro Alberto Guimarães, the great house went through a judicious restoration that reestablished its original architectural grandeur, and the gardens were beautified through an ambitious landscaping project that made use of a large volume of water from the Flores River, which cuts through the plantation. The garden's royal palms and ancient jaboticaba trees are a priceless legacy of the past.

In recent years Chacrinha has had a new owner, Sérgio Sahione Fadel, who respects its history and has not only preserved it faithfully but also enriched its possessions and increased its beauty. One of the most important art collectors in the country, Fadel incorporated part of his collection into the decor of the great house, the only condition being that the paintings be by Brazilian artists or by foreign artists who painted Brazilian themes. The fazenda holds some twenty works, predominantly those of nineteenth-century landscapists. Fadel has also expanded the breeding of dairy cattle, introducing purebred Jersey cows and the production of special milk packaged on the plantation. Another growing activity is a program for the breeding of long-maned pacers.

SECRETÁRIO

Secretário, seen here from the entrance to the garden, is the finest example of the neoclassical style as it was adapted to rural houses in Rio de Janeiro province. The symmetrically positioned triangular gables and handsomely crowned windows lend it an elegant refinement.

"We were riding along on our donkeys. The beautiful monotone of the countryside finally turned me completely over to inner meditations. . . . I was musing like that, with no great intimate disquiet but with that secret despair of those who have lost their homeland, when my animal, picking up the pace, seemed to sense the Tuileries. It was a plantation, Secretário.

"Cast your eyes on that superb dwelling. . . . The sun and Vitor Frond had already painted it with its rich waterfall, its distant hillocks covered with coffee trees, which a man, one single man, had put together in the course of twenty years of work. The Baron of Campo Belo, there in person was the first Montmorency."

So wrote Charles Ribeyrolles, a French exile in Brazil, describing his first sight of Secretário in the distance on a ride from Vassouras at the peak of the coffee boom in the year 1858. The memory of the Tuileries, the palace of the kings of France, rose up out of the lush gardens. Indeed, Secretário was the most eloquent illustration of a coffee plantation in every sense: a large house, immense coffee plantings, a respectable baron.

The architecture of the dwelling is neoclassical—the style introduced into Brazil just as the mansion was being planned. The two triangular gables at either end of the façade, exceptional in every detail, suggest its division into three units. The one on the right was occupied by the chapel. The one on the left held the family quarters above and the service areas below. Between them, on both floors, were the rich salons, their walls decoratively

painted or covered in fine imported wallpaper. Near the house is a French clock tower, marking the passage of time right up to the present.

The Secretário of today is not too different from the one that enthralled Ribeyrolles. There stands the imposing great house, surrounded by the restored gardens with their fountains and pools. The turbulent Secretário River, which cuts through the plantation, plunges over a waterfall near the house. The air that the visitor breathes inside and out encourages meditation on the past. The atmosphere is one of intense nostalgia.

Secretário has its origins in a land grant awarded in 1743 to Pedro Saldanha e Albuquerque and later transferred to Bartolomeu Machado Ferreira and Manuel Gomes Leal. The latter built the property's first modest residence, which would later make way for the mansion. It is thought that the name of the plantation comes from one of its early owners, who was secretary to the governor of the captaincy for a long time.

The great lord of Secretário, however, was Laureano Correa e Castro, honored with the title Baron of Campo Belo. It was he who built the beautiful house and the lovely gardens. It was he who covered the fazenda's vast, fertile fields with coffee groves, making Secretário the most important plantation in Vassouras during the cycle.

Inventories describe the interior of the mansion as being appointed with French furnishings and tall, gilt-framed mirrors. On the marble tops of tables and consoles stood fine porcelain jars and vases and bronze candelabra with chimneys of etched crystal. The dining room featured a large table that seated forty-eight, four sideboards, and a grandfather clock wound by a crank. The list of utensils was nothing short of princely: three chests of silverware, two smaller chests of gold-plated silver, fifty-six plates of worked silver, another twenty-four of silver with a smooth surface, and silver platters, salad bowls, pepper mills, and fruit dishes. In one of the salons, portraits of family members and of their imperial majesties lined the walls.

In Vassouras, a village founded in 1833 and elevated to the status of city in 1857, Campo Belo became a prominent figure. He and his brothers had inherited a fortune based on gold in Minas Gerais from their father, Francisco José Teixeira, Baron of Itambé. Instead of squandering it in the city, they increased it through planting. His brother Antônio, Baron of Tinguá, had the honor of playing host to Emperor Pedro II on a visit to Vassouras in 1848. Laureano himself served as a commander in the National Guard, and, as historian Inácio Raposo writes, his "military bearing impressed all who had the privilege of seeing him erect upon a fiery steed commanding his troops."

The Baron of Campo Belo died in Vassouras in 1861, leaving the plantation to his widow and his eldest son, Cristóvão Correa e Castro. The

need to improve the coffee plantings, acquire efficient machinery, and pay debts incurred in the purchase of other plantations forced the owners to mortgage Secretário to the Bank of Brazil. Cristóvão managed to pay off a large part of the debt, but his efforts were thwarted by the abolition of slavery and the end of the coffee cycle in Rio de Janeiro. After Cristóvão's death in 1905, his son and heir, Júlio Correa e Castro, renegotiated the mortgage but lost the plantation nevertheless in 1908. From then on Secretário belonged successively to Damphna Josephine Berthe Boogaests, Geraldo Rocha, Rural Colonization, Inc., and Mario Kröeff. Kröeff, the owner from 1952 to 1986, arranged for the division of the land among his three children, keeping the house and two hundred acres. This historic property, located fifteen miles from Vassouras, was bought by Martha Ribeiro de Britto in 1986.

Martha has undertaken the restoration of Secretário's famed garden and great house. The frescoes on the walls of the public rooms are

ABOVE: In the kitchen bunches of green bananas, the most common Brazilian fruit, are piled up on a table in front of the refrigerator.

OPPOSITE: Crystal pine-cone finials adorn the banister of the elegantly curved double staircase.

being repaired, and the house is being furnished with a combination of period and modern pieces. The chapel, which had been transformed into living quarters, has been returned to its original function. Thanks to Martha Britto's determination and enthusiasm, Secretário is again becoming one of the most magnificent plantation houses in all of Brazil.

RETIRO

The façade of Retiro's palatial great house is painted in exactly the same color as that of the Imperial Palace of Pedro II, now a museum in the neighboring city of Petrópolis.

Among all the great houses built during the Rio coffee cycle, Retiro is one of the few that achieved the sense of monumentality inherent in the architectural style that predominated at the time. Completed in 1869, it is in fact a two-story palace, a jewel of harmony and balance.

Located seven miles from Bemposta, a district of the town of Três Rios, Retiro, like so many other plantations in the Paraíba valley, was originally part of a much larger plantation that was divided and subdivided as the coffee culture developed. Its story is but one chapter in the saga of the Werneck family. One of the branches of the large family was the Santos Werneck clan. They came from the region of Vassouras to Paraíba do Sul in the third and fourth decades of the nineteenth century.

In 1837 Antônio Luís dos Santos Werneck—son of the pioneer Antônio Luís dos Santos and grandson of the patriarch, Inácio de Souza Werneck— acquired from Antônio Barroso Pereira an area of virgin forest that was ideal for growing coffee in what is today the district of Bemposta. This was not the first transaction between the two men; Antônio Luís was gradually becoming master of a vast holding in Paraíba do Sul, where his first plantation was originally called Boa Vista, and later Boa União.

Antônio Luís's wife, Ana Maria da Assunção, who had married him as a widow, died in 1844. At the time Antônio Luís was living with a step-daughter, Maria Delfina, and his own ten children—one of whom, Inácio, would become the Baron of Bemposta—on the prosperous fazenda Santo

Antônio de Massambará, which, along with neighboring São Francisco and São Fernando (see pages 76–83), founded by his brothers, were the most important in the Vassouras region.

The inventory taken upon Ana Maria's death reveals Antônio Luís's apprehension that discord might erupt among his many children after his own death. Long experienced in the reverses of a colonizer's life, he felt that the well-established Santo Antônio de Massambará plantation was, by its very nature, indivisible. Therefore, in 1846 he decided to turn it over to his nephew José de Souza Werneck and move to Paraíba do Sul with his children, where he set himself up on his Boa União plantation. While still alive he allotted a portion of his vast holdings in the area to each child so that each could found his or her own plantation. Unfortunately, Antônio

OPPOSITE: *The palm tree–lined entrance drive passes through the lush garden and ends in the courtyard of the residence.*

RIGHT: *Some two hundred towering royal palms, planted by landscape designer Roberto Burle Marx, give Retiro's garden its distinction. This highly ornamental tree was brought to Brazil by King John VI in 1808. He planted the Palma Mater (the mother of all palm trees) in the Botanical Garden of Rio de Janeiro. That tree reached its 150th birthday before being struck by lightning.*

Luís dos Santos Werneck died in 1848 and did not live to see the extraordinary coffee groves that would bring so much wealth to his descendants and so much progress and civilization to that part of the valley.

The fazenda Retiro arose on the portion of land that fell to Antônio Luís's daughter Geraldina das Chagas. In those days, marriage between cousins and in-laws was a common practice, encouraged and sometimes even demanded by the coffee civilization's patriarchal system. So it was not unusual that when Geraldina's first husband, Guilherme de Araújo Franco, died, she then married her cousin and brother-in-law Manuel Luís dos Santos Werneck, the widower of her half-sister, Maria Delfina. Manuel Luís and Geraldina built Retiro's beautiful seat. After Manuel Luís's death in 1874 the prosperous plantation went to his daughter Thereza, who was married to the physician Mário Nunes Galvão.

At the end of the coffee cycle, when disillusioned planters began selling off their fazendas, Retiro was bought by the Moreira and Macedo families. Linked by marriage, members of these families lived and worked on the plantation for several generations, until it was acquired by Eduardo Pessôa de Queiroz and his wife, Luiza, under whose ownership the third phase of the property began. When Eduardo and Luiza purchased it, the great house was in a sorry state of disrepair, and all of its original furnishings were gone. In the 1980s the couple undertook a careful, thorough renovation of the house, both inside and out, remaining faithful to the imposing yet graceful lines of its original architecture. They oversaw the restoration of the delicate murals in the chapel and appointed the interior with nineteenth-century furnishings that are in keeping with the architecture, as well as with modern conveniences. In pride of place is an 1881 oil painting by German artist Georg Grimm that depicts Retiro at the height of the coffee cycle (see page 15). Surrounding the house is a magnificent garden, featuring some two hundred royal palms, that was designed by world-renowned landscape designer Roberto Burle Marx.

Eduardo has also preserved the outbuildings that line Retiro's classic "quadrilateral"; the original warehouses, granaries, and slave

OPPOSITE: *In the main entrance hall the cobblestone floor is laid out in a pattern of intersecting circles. A copy of Velázquez's portrait of Charles V hangs on the wall.*

BELOW: *A lithograph of Eduardo Pessôa de Queiroz's great-grandfather hangs above a nineteenth-century clerk's desk in the entrance hall.*

OPPOSITE: *In this hallway on the second floor the modern wallpaper and rugs beautifully complement the traditional nineteenth-century furnishings.*

RIGHT: *Upper part of the chapel altar. The layout of the Retiro chapel (two stories high with its own entrance) is typical of the chapels in large coffee-plantation houses.*

quarters now house the dairy cows—a mixture of zebus of the Gir breed with black-and-white Dutch cattle—whose breeding is the plantation's main activity today. The greater part of Retiro's 1,400 acres is covered with various pasture grasses. Permanent agricultural and veterinary services on the property assure it the status of a model fazenda of its kind.

Thanks to the efforts of Luiza and Eduardo Pessôa de Queiroz, Retiro ranks as one of the most beautiful rural houses in Brazil.

RIO NOVO

T he European chalet style was introduced to Brazil during the first half of the nineteenth century in cities colonized by German immigrants, such as Petrópolis and Friburgo in Rio province. These urban chalets were sophisticated but not ostentatious in their treatment of the style, the characteristic feature of which is elaborate, carved-wood "lacework" decorating eaves and balconies.

At the end of this corridor, which runs the length of the house, is an oil painting of Marshal Deodoro da Fonseca proclaiming the birth of the Republic of Brazil on November 15, 1889.

In the last quarter of the coffee cycle the chalet style was often adopted in the construction of rural houses. The plantation house at Rio Novo, four miles from the town of Paraíba do Sul, is a fine example of the style in a rural setting. Other plantation houses of the type, such as Santa Luiza in Rio das Flores, to mention one that is still standing, went overboard in their treatment of the style, a tendency that can be explained by the eccentric and sometimes exhibitionist personalities of the coffee barons.

The work of architect Pierre Pézerat, a member of the French mission that came to Brazil to do remodeling work on the Imperial Palace in Rio de Janeiro, Rio Novo differs in certain respects from traditional chalets: for instance, its balcony is atypical of the style, and its chapel is a separate structure adjoined to the house, a configuration more typical of sugar-plantation houses. Despite these divergences, however, it basically adheres to the chalet style.

Like so many other plantations, Rio Novo came into being as a result of the breakup of a larger property. As Pedro Gomes da Silva, the historian of Paraíba do Sul, would say, it is an "offspring" plantation. Originally, its land was part of a grant to Garcia Rodrigues Paes, the builder of the New Road to

ABOVE: *Hats, whips, reins, and a horn, all necessities of plantation life, hang from a rack in the entrance hall.*

RIGHT: *A fine cane settee made during the Empire is ironically positioned right beneath the painting that depicts the event that brought the Empire to an end.*

OPPOSITE: *A simple wooden cabinet lends a rustic charm to the entrance.*

Minas Gerais, who received it as a royal gift for his services to the Portuguese Crown in the eighteenth century.

A descendant of Garcia Paes, Pedro Dias Leme da Câmara, named a baron by King John VI in 1818 and elevated to Marquis of São João Marcos by Dom Pedro I in 1826, was the owner of the lands in 1845, when he sold them to Ana Rosa de Jesus and her son, João Antônio de Araújo e Silva. João Antônio married Maria da Trindade Araújo, the future baroness of Rio Novo plantation, and they had many children but only one son, Pedro Antônio by name, who as "Pedro Araújo" would become quite famous for his courage and boldness in defending the interests of the poor.

Lacking the capital for essential investments, João Antônio and Maria were forced to go into debt, and the situation worsened when João Antônio died. Maria then married Miguel Ribeiro de Sá, a Portuguese citizen and former partner of the wealthy Viscount of Entre Rios, a large landowner in the region (see São Lourenço, pages 98–103). With determination and hard work,

Miguel was able to turn the plantation into a profitable coffee producer, and he gave it the beautiful great house that serves as its seat to this day. In 1882 the imperial government awarded him the title Baron of Ribeiro de Sá.

A man of exceptional integrity, the baron easily formed influential friendships that promoted him into the political life of the province, and he became one of the most notable figures in the development of Paraíba do Sul. Dividing his time between his plantation and the town, he eventually held all the public offices in Paraíba do Sul, where he built a mansion that now houses the Cultural Center of the municipality.

Under his administration Rio Novo reached its greatest prosperity. Supported by the plantation's outstanding production of coffee, the owners enjoyed a high style of life. Important neighboring plantations included São Lourenço, owned by the Viscount of Entre Rios, and Cantagalo, which belonged to Mariana Claudina Barroso Pereira de Carvalho, Countess of

The great house at Rio Novo was built by French architect Pierre Pézerat in the chalet style, which was introduced to Brazil by German immigrants and became quite widespread in the nineteenth century. The chapel is a separate structure, but it is adjoined to the house, an arrangement that was rare for plantation houses in the province of Rio de Janeiro. The "lacework" decorating the eaves of the gable is a typical feature of chalet style, while the statues on the platband of the roof add a neoclassical touch.

This bedroom features an Empire-style bed dating from the first half of the nineteenth century.

Rio Novo, a worthy aristocrat of Paraíba do Sul. On her lands, part of which was given to her slaves, the town of Entre Rios, today Três Rios, was founded.

When Baron Miguel died in 1904, his only son, José Lino Ribeiro de Sá, succeeded him on the plantation. By then the golden age had already come to an end, and from that point on Rio Novo had a succession of owners: the Landsberg family; the journalist José Soares Maciel Filho, celebrated as the author of the testament-letter of President Getúlio Vargas on his suicide in 1954—an important document in modern Brazilian history; Ney Galvão, a minister of the treasury, followed by his son, Mário Galvão; and finally the publisher Sérgio Carlos Abruzini Lacerda. In purchasing Rio Novo, the late Lacerda was the first to rekindle interest in preserving the old plantations of the valley, and his restoration of the house turned it into one of the most beautiful seats in the state of Rio de Janeiro. The modernizations he introduced, such as the installation of bathrooms, had the merit of not affecting the original structure or appearance of the residence. The interiors, decorated with eighteenth-century Bahian furniture and nineteenth-century pieces from Rio province, retain a rustic charm.

Now administered by Sérgio's heirs—Rosângela, Carlos Augusto, and their brothers—Rio Novo's 1,555 acres are a fine breeding site for Dutch dairy cows, which produce milk of superior quality.

SANTO ANTÔNIO DO PAIOL

Rear view of the great house, showing its U-shaped construction. The public rooms and chapel are located in the center; the service areas, including pantry, kitchen, lunchroom, and supply room, are on the left; and the bedrooms are on the right.

Santo Antônio do Paiol, located five miles from the town of Valença, was one of many fazendas founded on lands belonging to the vast Santa Tereza grant. The area was settled in the late eighteenth century, when forests were still being cleared and colonists were constantly skirmishing with the Coroado Indians—the true owners of the land. To quell the hostilities, the viceroy of Portugal in Brazil set up an Indian reservation, which today is the district known as Conservatória. Shortly after being confined to this reservation, the Indians were decimated by illnesses contracted through contact with whites.

Santo Antônio do Paiol's original house was built in 1804, and it was as rustic as the men who then occupied the region. The first owner was Francisco Martins Pimentel, a Portuguese from the Azores. In the early years Pimentel dedicated himself to subsistence farming. In the 1820s Manuel Antônio Esteves arrived in Brazil from Portugal and became a prosperous merchant in Vassouras. In 1848 he established relations with the Pimentel family, and two years later he married Pimentel's daughter Francisca, receiving as a dowry the plantation Santo Antônio do Paiol, just as the coffee cycle was entering its most prosperous phase. Shortly after the wedding Esteves's father-in-law died, and with his wealth increased, Esteves ordered the building of a new house, which was finished in 1852. He also expanded his coffee groves, acquiring or establishing new fazendas, such as São Manuel, Ribeirão, Santa Catarina, São Francisco, Nazaré, and Boa Vista. He was soon master of more than six hundred slaves and the leading citizen of Valença. Eliminating intermediaries, he handled production himself, establishing the export firm

of Esteves and Sons, which operated out of Rio de Janeiro and Santos. Thus, in addition to being a great plantation owner, he became a major coffee merchant. He also helped fund the construction of the União Valenciana railway, which connected Valença to the trunk line of the Dom Pedro II railway and thereby to Rio and São Paulo, with obvious benefits for the local economy.

Manuel Antônio Esteves died in 1879 at the height of his prestige, leaving his fortune to his children. He was succeeded in his business operations by his son Francisco Martins Esteves. A person of great refinement, Francisco lived for a time in Paris, where he married Ana Carolina, the daughter of the minister-counselor of the Empire, Zacarias de Goes e Vasconcelos. Returning to Brazil, he took over the business, but without showing any liking or aptitude for the world of commerce. Administering the plantations as best he could, given the difficulties that ensued as the coffee cycle went into decline, Francisco acquired the shares of the other heirs and settled permanently on Santo Antônio do Paiol. He ran it jointly with his son, Marcos Zacarias Manuel Esteves, who eventually succeeded him.

During this third and last phase of Esteves family ownership, Marcos was forced to sell off part of the land to insure the maintenance of the rest of the property. After he died in 1941, his widow, Francisca Olympia Alves de Queiroz Esteves, fought long and hard to preserve what was left of the fazenda, although it was virtually inactive and brought in no income. But by 1969, unable to continue any longer, unable even to support herself, she decided to donate the fazenda's land to a religious organization, the Congregation of the Small Works of Divine Providence (Don Orione), and she now lies buried in the ancient cemetery of Santo Antônio do Paiol, alongside the pioneer Francisco Martins Pimental and his great-grandson Marcos.

Respecting the wishes of its benefactor, the Congregation wisely built new lodgings for its meetings and spiritual retreats, leaving the original structures on the fazenda untouched. The great house and everything else, including the memory of the Esteves family, is under the care of the present owners, Rogério Luís and Maria Alice Vianna, who have faithfully restored the house and rescued the fazenda's historical legacy.

In the course of their painstaking, three-year restoration of the great house, the Viannas not only reconstructed the original architectural features but also repaired its valuable furniture, which had been stored away in the cellars of the house. These pieces now occupy public rooms and bedrooms once more. Oil portraits of Esteves family members were taken out of their hiding places under beds and restored; they now decorate the walls of the rooms just as they did in the nineteenth century. The fazenda's rare library was inventoried and its volumes were replaced on the shelves of a cabinet built specially for that purpose. Consisting of French, English, Portuguese, and Brazilian books, periodicals, and documents, the library reveals fascinating information about imperial Brazil, about the mansions of the Esteves family, and about the commercial life of the plantation, including the administration of coffee sales and the control of slaves. The Viannas deserve much credit for having unearthed this valuable repository and for making it available to scholars.

Bougainvillea beautifies the courtyard entrance to the service wing.

This view of the bedroom wing clearly shows that the house is a one-story structure with a "high" basement in front and a "low" one in the rear. The garden, a part of which can be seen here, is thought to be the work of the renowned French garden designer Auguste Glaziou, who created the most beautiful public gardens in imperial Rio de Janeiro and worked in Valença at the height of the coffee cycle.

At present, Santo Antônio do Paiol is devoted to the raising of purebred Jersey dairy cows on 350 acres of land, using the most advanced techniques, including the implantation of embryos for reproduction. On its pastures a herd of the Canchim breed grazes, a type obtained by crossing the European Charolais breed with Indian zebus of the Nelore breed. The females of the Canchim breed are the recipients of the Jersey embryos. The milk produced is processed on the fazenda and distributed to retail dealers.

A small coffee grove re-creates the atmosphere that reigned on the fazenda in the past. A production station for cuttings used in reforestation is being organized in an effort to compensate for the devastating effects of the clear-cutting that took place during the coffee cycle. In addition, the fazenda is moving toward setting up visits by interested groups. Rogério Vianna is one of the founders of the nongovernmental organization Preservale, whose purpose is to develop interest in ecology and tourism, and to preserve the legacy of the Paraíba do Sul River valley.

UBÁ

The dining room at Ubá is furnished with nineteenth-century pieces of various styles.

T he name Ubá, as we are told by Saint-Hilaire in his *Second Trip from Rio de Janeiro to Minas,* means "a tall species of grass that grows along the water's edge and is common in the region of the Paraíba do Sul River." Although the Ubá land grant, like that of Pau Grande, was awarded in the eighteenth century, it was not settled or used by anyone but the "wild Indians" mentioned by Saint-Hilaire until José Rodrigues da Cruz sold his share in Pau Grande and, moving to the bank of the Paraíba River in 1801, founded the Ubá plantation. Making every effort to live in peace with the natives, José Rodrigues da Cruz won their cooperation and respect by treating them well and generously supplying them with food. The Indians called him the "Old Captain." Chief Bocamã was especially devoted to him, and the landowner might have realized his dream of a colony of peaceful, hard-working natives if Bocamã had not died young, leaving his people confused and at the mercy of the neighboring Portuguese, who abused them and infected them with diseases that decimated them.

Ubá's lands stretched along the lush, wild valley of the Paraíba do Sul River, from the environs of the New Road to Minas Gerais all the way to the no less beautiful region bathed by the Paraibuna River and its tributary, the Preto. José Cruz's task was to turn this huge tract of virgin territory into a productive plantation. Its main crops were sugar cane, corn, and manioc, and from its earliest years Ubá served as an important supplier of basic necessities to travelers between Rio de Janeiro and Minas Gerais. Cruz's ownership did not last long, however. He no doubt had his reasons for selling the plantation in 1806 to his nephew João Rodrigues Pereira de Almeida, who built the beautiful great house that stands there to this day.

Under João Rodrigues's administration the fazenda became a pioneering coffee-growing establishment in the valley. His successful cultivation of the little red berry created such a stir in the capital that in 1828 Dom Pedro I (who later became Pedro IV of Portugal) awarded him the title Baron of Ubá. According to exiled French writer Charles Ribeyrolles, the baron "was not merely a farmer. He was a scholar and a member of high society. Dom Pedro I had made him Baron of Ubá for services to the nation, and it was he whom Saint-Hilaire saluted in his writings for the courteous hospitality granted him during such pleasant days." As Saint-Hilaire writes about Ubá: "During my sojourn in Brazil, nowhere did I spend happier moments. Every day I took long excursions in the forests and along the riverbanks, coming upon many

RIGHT: *The late landscape designer Roberto Burle Marx created this flower arrangement a few days before his death.*

OPPOSITE: *The shuttered window inset into the door of this bedroom is typical of the colonial style, as are the lattice doors of the cupboard.*

things I came to know, and I dedicated myself to my work without any of the privations that were so often painful during my travels."

The Baron of Ubá's life is a striking example of how coffee money changed the habits and customs of people and families. While the original masters of Ubá had been relatively crude and uneducated, the Baron of Ubá was sociable and well-mannered; he appeared at court regularly, negotiated loans in Europe in 1821, and owned a mansion in Rio de Janeiro that later became a bird museum and then served as the National Archives. The Baron of Ubá died in 1830 and the fazenda passed on to his son, José Pereira de Almeida. José lived there until his death in 1874 and was, therefore, master of the establishment during the peak of the coffee cycle.

Throughout most of the twentieth century the fazenda belonged to a traditional agricultural enterprise called Companhia Centros Pastoris, but in the 1970s it passed to José Luís de Magalhães Lins and his wife, Nininha. When they acquired it, Ubá was in a deteriorated state, and its historic sugar mill and slave quarters were beyond repair. But they completely restored the

OPPOSITE: *Built before the coffee cycle, the great house at Ubá has a large veranda that runs the length of its front façade, a feature typical of sugar-plantation houses.*

BELOW: *At the main entrance, elegantly shaped stone steps lead to the veranda, with its whimsically carved balustrade.*

OPPOSITE: *Amid the ancient mango trees in Ubá's picturesque garden, a string of hammocks beckons invitingly.*

RIGHT: *Another of Burle Marx's flower arrangements adorns the veranda, which is comfortably furnished with wicker tables and armchairs.*

great house, exercising good taste and great respect for its original design. Built at the beginning of the nineteenth century in the style predominant on eighteenth-century sugar plantations, it has an imposing veranda along the front façade featuring an artistically carved wooden balustrade.

Behind the house the new owners built another house in the same style to accommodate the kitchen, pantries, laundry, and other service rooms. The original house remains authentic, holding reception rooms and bedrooms. With its trellised and shuttered windows, the interior decor has an eighteenth-century feel. The garden, with its extensive lawns, flower beds, plants, and ornamental trees, seems to rise up out of nowhere. Located fifteen miles from the municipality of Vassouras, of which it is part, Ubá covers six thousand acres—a sizable area for these times. Its main activity today is the breeding of prize cattle.

SÃO FERNANDO

The long, narrow dining room at São Fernando is furnished in the classic manner of nineteenth-century coffee plantations. A Portuguese tradition, the large, many-leaved table was a constant in Brazilian rural houses. Equally traditional is the set of oval-backed, round-seated cane chairs.

Situated less than a mile from Massambará, a district in the municipality of Vassouras, is São Fernando, one of the great coffee fazendas that survived the cycle. Today its fields have been turned over to the raising of Holstein-Frisian dairy cattle and pacers.

Its origins date back to the eighteenth century, when a part of the Sertão da Varzia, or Vargem Grande, and Vila Latina land grants was awarded to Portuguese captain José Luís dos Santos. Upon his death, José Luís's land was inherited by his oldest son, Antônio Luís dos Santos, also a grantee, who combined his own territory with his father's to form the basis of the fazenda São Fernando.

Antônio married one of the many daughters of Inácio de Souza Werneck—patriarch of the Wernecks, who after being widowed was ordained a priest in the presence of his twelve children—and became the founder of the Santos Wernecks, a family of illustrious plantation owners and noblemen. His son Fernando Luís dos Santos Werneck founded and gave his name to the São Fernando fazenda. In 1813 his territory was enlarged by the fazenda Alferes, an inheritance from his mother.

Fernando Luís and his wife, Maria Luiza Barbosa, had four children. Maria Luiza died in childbirth in 1825; the inventory taken after her death indicates that the plantation's income and holdings were still quite modest. Fernando subsequently remarried, and his second wife, Jesuína Polucena, the daughter of the owners of Mangalarga plantation, bore him twelve children, all of whom became prominent figures in Rio coffee society. Fernando Luís and his many children built the great house and developed the plantation, which reached its height in size and coffee production in the 1850s. That it was one of the most prosperous coffee fazendas in the Paraíba valley is evident from an inventory taken at the time of Fernando Luís's death in 1850; it lists high-quality furnishings, silver cutlery with ivory handles, porcelain, crystal, and much gold and silver jewelry.

This inventory also paints a fascinating picture of the conventions of the period. Lighting was provided by copper candlesticks and sconces, porcelain lamps, brass hanging lamps, and iron lanterns. In lieu of indoor plumbing, there were chamber pots and jars, as well as bedpans with or without covers, white or colored, and encased in stools or benches.

After five months of widowhood, Jesuína Polucena married the Spaniard Juan Arsenio Moreira Serra in the plantation oratory. Concerned with the education of his stepchildren, the new master of São Fernando provided the house with a wide-ranging library and introduced such tools

of learning as binoculars and a pantograph. In addition, he reorganized the administration of the plantation, making it run more efficiently. For instance, he insisted on feeding and taking better care of the slaves, not out of pity but as a way of increasing production; he continued to use instruments of torture, however, such as the "tree trunk for blacks" installed by Fernando Luís. When Jesuína died in 1855, she left half the estate to Arsenio, and he enlarged the holdings, enriched the house and embellished it with gardens, built new service structures, and installed steam power. The fazenda's coffee groves and production grew until his death in 1865.

The sole heiress, his stepdaughter Guilhermina Leopoldina d'Oliveira Werneck, immediately sold the plantation to Mathias Bernardino Alexandre, who in turn sold it, two years later, to José Ferreira Neves. The latter, settling

ABOVE: *One of the guest bedrooms in the public wing of the house.*

on the plantation with his family, was not fortunate in the enterprise because he had bought it at the moment of the coffee cycle's downturn. Like so many other plantation owners, Neves went deeply into debt trying to reverse the slide, but he died in 1879 without having paid off his bank loans and with the plantation mortgaged. His widow married José Benedito Marcondes Machado, who could not prevent the mortgage from being foreclosed. From mortgage to mortgage and foreclosure to foreclosure São Fernando went through two more owners, and neither they nor their heirs could hold back the fazenda's inexorable decline.

In 1948, reduced to 575 acres and in a deteriorated state, São Fernando was bought by Paulino Barroso Salgado, who intended to turn it into a resort. Without fulfilling his dream he sold the fazenda to Pedro Alberto Guimarães in 1980, who undertook its restoration. In 1983, its size increased to 1,300 acres, the plantation changed hands again. The present owner, Ronaldo César Coelho, not only finished the restoration but also enriched the decor and furnishings of the great house. Deeply interested in the history of the coffee cycle and believing that it would be unfair to deny access to others interested in the subject and in the beauty of old fazendas, Coelho has opened São Fernando to visitors. He is even considering setting up a foundation to maintain and perpetuate the property as a historical landmark.

VENEZA

Veneza is typical of the architectural eclecticism prevalent during the coffee cycle. The fanlights above the windows are Luso-Brazilian, while the strictly symmetrical placement of the windows is neoclassical. Like many other plantation houses, it was built as a one-story dwelling over a "high" basement.

T he oldest land grants awarded in the backlands of what is today the city of Valença date from the 1770s, but use of the land did not take place immediately, primarily because of the resistance put up by local Indian tribes. In the case of Conservatória, the district of Valença where the fazenda Veneza is located, colonization suffered an even greater delay because the region had been chosen by the Portuguese Crown for the confinement of the indigenous population, whose hostile actions were impeding the establishment of the town of Valença. First designated Santo Antônio do Rio Bonito, where the *conservatório dos índios* (Indian reservation) was created, with the passage of time the district lost its original name and became known simply as Conservatória. Thus Veneza was not established as a coffee plantation until the 1800s. Curiously, the fazenda next to Veneza is called Florença. The two plantations had no connection to each other, so one can only wonder why their founders gave them the names of famous Italian cities.

The first owner of Veneza was Manuel Gomes de Carvalho, Baron of Amparo. A native of Santiago de Amorim, Portugal, where he was born at the end of the eighteenth century, Manuel emigrated to Brazil at the dawn of the coffee cycle in the Paraíba valley. A strong-willed man of action—like so many of the coffee pioneers—in a few years he became a wealthy and prestigious plantation owner in the town of Barra Mansa, especially in the Amparo district—whence his title of nobility—where he established his first plantation, Santana do Turvo. Veneza did not belong to the baron for long. His many activities in the province, in the capital, and on various fazendas in

ABOVE: *An eighteenth-century Brazilian bench adorns one of the parlors. Its back is decoratively carved, and its curved arms end in volutes.*

OPPOSITE: *This charming, chalet-style structure used to be the building where coffee beans were processed. All the machinery is now gone, and the interior has been decorated as a salon. A celebration marking the reopening of the plantation after its restoration was held here.*

the Amparo district far from Conservatória led him to get rid of the plantation before his death in 1855.

There are no trustworthy reports detailing the history of the construction of Veneza's great house. Even inventories, the most reliable source, can be imprecise in their information. What can be deduced is that the house was built by the baron without any great concern for its architecture, as he did not live there but at Santana do Turvo. The great owner of Veneza, beginning in the 1870s, was Francisco Paulo de Almeida, Baron of Guaraciaba. Between the two barons there were several other owners. The probability is that the house underwent enlargements during the height of the coffee cycle and that its appearance by the end of the century was the work of Guaraciaba.

The L-shaped great house was built as a one-story dwelling over a high basement. Of simplified neoclassical architecture, it displays the eclecticism prevalent during the cycle. Particularly noteworthy are the elegantly patterned stained-glass fanlights above the double-sash windows on the upper level—a Luso-Brazilian feature.

Veneza went through a long period of abandonment in the twentieth century, a time when many of the old plantation houses, considered much too large and expensive to maintain, were torn down by their owners, who used the excellent materials to build much smaller new ones. Fortunately, Veneza did not share that fate during the decades that it was owned by Gabriel Vilela and his successors. The fazenda "hibernated" until 1970, when it was acquired by the journalist Horácio Gomes Leite de Carvalho Júnior, who undertook the restoration of the property, to which he was sentimentally attached: the first Baron of Amparo was his great-grandfather and the second Baron of Amparo, Joaquim Gomes Leite de Carvalho, was his grandfather and also the person who had reared him from early childhood.

Horácio took great pleasure in restoring old coffee plantations. Aided by his wife, Lily Monique, he restored, in addition to his great-grandfather's fazendas Veneza and Santana do Turvo, Paraíso, Rio Branco, and two others. He was in the process of starting up new restoration projects when he died. Veneza remains the property of Lily Monique de Carvalho Marinho, who married another journalist, Roberto Marinho, owner of the Globo organization.

The building that housed coffee-processing machinery has also been restored. Although the machines are gone, the water wheel that ran them is

RIGHT: One of the bedrooms has been converted into a bathroom without altering the original wall decor, floor, or door. The screen was made in Brazil after a late-eighteenth-century French model.

still in working order, and the large, open room has been decorated as a salon, where festivities on the fazenda now take place.

Veneza is dedicated to raising beef and dairy cattle. There is a medium-sized coffee grove, prized within its present limits. There is also an officially controlled zoo devoted to the breeding of several endangered species.

Located four miles from Conservatória, with an area of 5,500 acres, the Veneza plantation has reforested part of its lands with pines and eucalyptus trees. The beautiful view from the house is quite different from that of the virgin forest of times gone by, but in some ways recalls the landscape first seen by the Baron of Amparo, which destiny has returned into the hands of his descendants.

BONSUCESSO

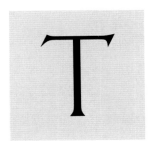

Bonsucesso's magnificent three-story great house, reflected in the water. The palm trees flanking the entrance drive are a recent addition.

OVERLEAF: *An exquisite symmetry gives the solid house built at the height of the coffee cycle an austere elegance.*

The fazenda Bonsucesso is located four miles from the municipality of Cordeiro, an area that in colonial times was part of the jurisdiction of the town of Cantagalo. In the early nineteenth century it was rumored that the virginal and uninhabited Cantagalo region was rich in veins of easily extractable gold. As the word spread, people began flooding into the area, hoping to strike it rich. Among them was Jacques, or Jacob, van Erven, a Dutch engineer who had fled to Rio de Janeiro in 1824 to avoid arrest for his involvement in certain dubious political affairs in Europe. In 1830 Jacques and a Portuguese acquaintance, Antônio Clemente Pinto, set off for the Cantagalo mountains to prospect for gold. It is unlikely that they found any because the rumors of gold in Cantagalo proved false. Nevertheless, Antônio Clemente Pinto and Jacques van Erven stayed on in the mountains, becoming friends for life and wealthy coffee planters, fathering generations of plantation owners.

A legendary figure, Antônio became the first Baron of Friburgo. The owner of many plantations and many slaves, he built as his residence the mansion of Gavião in Cantagalo (the seat of the fazenda Gavião) and the luxurious Catete Palace in Rio de Janeiro. Van Erven was Antônio's constant collaborator in the administration of the complex. According to the German traveler Tschudi, the Dutchman "was the first to approach agriculture scientifically, introducing several innovations in agricultural technology." One of van Erven's inventions, a machine to benefit coffee growing, was registered with the Society for the Advancement of National Industry in Rio de Janeiro. To the Brazilian Historical and Geographical Institute he sent bones and

fossils found on his land to be studied. Van Erven married three times. His third wife bore him his only son, Antônio van Erven, who inherited the lands in the municipality of Cantagalo, where he founded the fazenda Nossa Senhora de Bonsucesso.

Judging from the date inscribed on the façade, the great house was finished in 1864. The owner of other important fazendas in the region, including Palmas and Santa Clara, Antônio gave Bonsucesso to his daughter Ana Clara when she married Antônio Faria de Salgado. She lived there with her family for the next thirty years, through the end of the Rio coffee cycle. Bonsucesso could not escape the difficulties that beset so many coffee fazendas during that period, and in 1914 the Van Ervens sold the plantation to Agenor

ABOVE: Delicate trompe l'oeil panels depicting European landscapes decorate the wall of the main staircase.

OPPOSITE: This parlor is furnished with a Louis-Philippe cane settee and a Dona Maria center table.

Monnerat, the descendant of a Swiss family who in 1808, at the invitation of King John VI of Portugal, had settled in high, cold Friburgo but later moved closer to Cantagalo, the more moderate climate of which was better suited for agriculture.

The new owners of Bonsucesso, traditional farmers, lived and worked on the plantation for many years. With the death of Agenor Monnerat in 1963, the fazenda, still a large property, was divided among his widow and children. The seat, consisting of about seven hundred acres, lay abandoned

ABOVE: *Past meets present as an ancient "singing" oxcart (so called for the deep, sharp tones produced by the wheels as they turn) crosses a recently built cement bridge.*

OPPOSITE: *The spacious kitchen, tastefully renovated with decorative tiles and marble-topped counters, retains the traditional open ceiling, which allowed smoke from wood-burning stoves to escape.*

until, in a deplorable state of preservation, it was bought by its present owner, Antônio Willemsens Neves da Rocha. Widespread and careful restoration has retrieved its singular splendor both inside and out.

The great house at Bonsucesso is eclectic in style. Its three-story structure—unique for a coffee-plantation house—has a simple, stately elegance. Locally manufactured nineteenth-century Brazilian furniture decorates its public rooms and bedrooms, and delicately painted murals depicting landscapes adorn the main interior stairwell. The breeding of purebred Suffolk sheep is the fazenda's principal activity, and the whole complex evokes the memory of a happy past.

SÃO LOURENÇO

When the gold mines of Minas Gerais began to peter out in the eighteenth century, José Rabelo de Macedo and his wife, Maria de Carvalho Duarte, decided to leave their town of São João d'El Rei and start a new life in a then sparsely inhabited part of Rio de Janeiro province. Accompanied by their daughter Mariana Jacinta de Macedo and her husband, Antônio Barroso Pereira, they arrived in the Paraíba do Sul River valley and settled down in Sebolas, a place near the New Road and the future site of the town Paraíba do Sul. During the height of the coffee cycle they became important producers, and Antônio was awarded the title Baron of Entre Rios.

The property founded by Rabelo was called Mato Grosso because of the presence of trees of extraordinary thickness in the virgin forest. When Rabelo died, the plantation was inherited by Antônio, who wisely used the money he had saved from his mining days to acquire new properties. Soon Mato Grosso was the largest plantation in the region. Antônio didn't even know exactly where his property ended. After his death, Mariana Jacinta remained in charge of the enormous holdings. When she remarried, her property, combined with that of her new husband, Colonel José Antônio Barbosa Teixeira, owner of the Sebolas plantation, comprised the entire eastern territory of the Paraíba do Sul River valley.

On these lands the colonel established the fazenda Bemposta for his stepson, Antônio. But in 1817 Antônio left Bemposta along with his mother and stepfather on receipt of the concession of Cantagalo, "a land grant in the backlands between the rivers Paraíba and Paraibuna," the site of the future

RIGHT: *The master bedroom is furnished with an intricately carved and turned Manueline-style Portuguese bed.*

OPPOSITE: *A pair of marble-topped sideboards decorate the hallway leading to the kitchen. Note the broad floorboards and sturdy shutters.*

town of Entre Rios, today called Três Rios. Four large plantations were founded on these lands, including Cachoeira, from whose breakup São Lourenço would be born.

São Lourenço was one of those coffee-producing establishments that paradoxically came into existence when the economy of the region was entering an irreversible decline. Unaware of the impending crisis, plantation owners blithely continued dividing and subdividing their lands—a practice that had proved useful in setting children up on their own and in decentralizing the administration of crops. They established rich new fazendas like São Lourenço precisely at a time when prudence would have advised moderation in investments and spending.

In 1877 Antônio Barroso Pereira Júnior, the second Baron of Entre Rios and a future viscount, built the beautiful seat of São Lourenço. Inspired by

ABOVE: *Relatively modest in size, the house at São Lourenço is a one-story residence over a basement sufficiently high to render it "inhabitable." Its architectural detailing, however, is exceptional, especially the stone quoins and pilasters punctuating the front façade, the window pediments, and the ironwork of the balconies and the basement vents.*

OPPOSITE: *The house, situated on a rise, overlooks the pool, which occupies part of the former* terreiro, *and the church tower.*

neoclassical models, yet exhibiting the eclecticism in vogue during the second half of the nineteenth century, its sophisticated stone masonry and fine wrought-iron balconies made it the most distinguished plantation house in the Paraíba valley. Situated prominently on a height, it commands a sweeping view of the surrounding landscape.

On the death of the Viscount of Entre Rios in 1906, the fazenda was sold by his heirs to Frederico d'Olne, a Belgian textile merchant who owned a neighboring plantation. Neither D'Olne nor his son and heir was interested in the seat of São Lourenço, so it remained closed and abandoned for many years until it was purchased by Maísa and Rodolfo Figueira de Melo. Conscious of the importance of preserving a piece of historical heritage, the couple faithfully restored the great house to its former elegance.

Located five miles from the town of Três Rios and consisting of 1,340 acres, São Lourenço's principal activity today is the raising of purebred Dutch dairy cows and riding horses. In addition to the crops necessary to feed the livestock, the plantation also grows coffee. Cultivated in accordance with the latest methods, the coffee grove revives the dream of a vanished era.

JURÉA

Juréa's pleasant veranda extends along a good part of the second floor of the house. The curious chairs with wheels were made in Petrópolis in 1940.

In 1850, at the height of the coffee cycle, when prosperous coffee plantations in Rio province were being established by the dozens, the Empire enacted a law to regularize the deeding of land. Creating the so-called "Parish Registry of Lands," the law delegated to parish churches the function of registrar of deeds. Book 63 of that registry, which was under the "responsibility of the vicar of the parish of Our Lady of the Sorrows of Piraí," contains the following protocol: "On October 21, 1855, I was presented with the deeds to the lands owned by His Excellency, the Baron of Piraí, and said deeds contain the following: The undersigned is the owner of two plantations in the Parish of Our Lady of the Sorrows, one known as Juréa, half a square league, bordered on one side by the Baron of Santa Isabel and his heirs, on another by the São Lourenço plantation, and on another by Mathias Gonçalves de Oliveira Roxo, whose half league of land was awarded by a Land-Grant Charter." The declaration is dated "Três Saltos, October 21, 1855," and signed "With the power of attorney from my father, His Excellency the Baron of Piraí, Joaquim Gonçalves de Morais."

The Baron of Piraí, José Gonçalves de Morais, was one of the largest landowners in the Paraíba valley. Três Saltos was his most important plantation. His son-in-law José Joaquim de Lima e Silva Sobrinho, the future Count of Tocantins, received the fazenda Juréa as a present on his marriage to Piraí's daughter Emiliana.

A military officer by training, José Joaquim figured prominently in imperial Brazil. Going into civilian life in the 1840s, he occupied positions of great social and political importance, including director of the Bank of Brazil

BELOW: *The second-floor hallway, with its two-toned "skirt-and-blouse" ceiling, is furnished with a grandfather clock made in Chicago in 1880, a John VI cane settee, and the coat of arms of the Portuguese Coelho Fragoso family, ancestors of the owner.*

OPPOSITE: *In the dining room the paintings flanking the fireplace are recent reproductions of portraits of Luíza and Maria da Glória, the paternal grandmother and maternal great-grandmother of the owner, respectively.*

and president of the Chamber of Commerce of Rio de Janeiro, known at the time as the Society of Members of the Exchange, a post he filled for twenty-three years.

With so many civic duties, the Count of Tocantins could not devote himself to the plantation he had received from his father-in-law, so he passed it on to his son Luís César de Lima e Silva, a diplomat married to Vera Haritoff, of an aristocratic Russian family. Luís César died young, in Paris, while serving as secretary of the Brazilian legation. Juréa was inherited by his children: Emiliana Rita, Ana, Helena, Maurício, and Leopoldo. According to an inventory taken in 1875, it can be estimated that the construction of the great house took place during the 1860s.

Time passed, the Empire fell, the nineteenth century gave way to the twentieth, and transfers among brothers and sisters left Maurício as sole owner in 1940. Unlike most plantations in the state of Rio, during all that time Juréa had continued to grow coffee along with other crops. The reason for this was that the owners not only did not live on the plantation but did not depend on its income, involved as they were in other activities in Rio de Janeiro and abroad. On Maurício's death his only son, Sérgio de Lima e Silva, inherited the plantation. Giving up a diplomatic career, he settled on the plantation, undertaking its restoration and developing a program of breeding dairy cattle.

In 1955 Juréa was acquired from the Lima e Silva family by Genésio Pires. During his tenure the chapel dedicated to Saint Sebastian was built and the breeding of dairy cattle remained the plantation's principal activity. In 1972 Genésio Pires transferred Juréa to his son José Carlos Fragoso Pires, the present owner, and about that time a government policy of fiscal incentives brought reforestation programs to the region. With the neighboring plantation of São José, which had been annexed by purchase, Juréa is now the site of three reforestation projects, which will eventually cover its fields with pine and eucalyptus trees and bring back various species of wild animals: anteaters, pacas, deer, siriemas, otters, and a great variety of birds such as iambus and jacus.

ABOVE: *Retaining its rustic ceiling beams and flagstone floor, the former basement warehouse has been transformed into comfortable guest quarters, where past and present mingle harmoniously. Hanging on the wall to the right is the fifteenth-century sonnet "Le Bonheur de ce monde" by Cristophe Plantin, appropriately describing the happiness a beautiful home can bring.*

OPPOSITE: *Juréa preserves the three classic elements of a coffee fazenda: great house, terreiro, and granary. Other outbuildings include coach houses, warehouses, a school, and an old distillery for cachaça, the national drink made from sugar cane.*

José Carlos, a breeder of thoroughbred racehorses in Rio Grande do Sul and current president of the Brazilian Jockey Club, has also developed a part of Juréa as a place for the rest, recuperation, and training of horses. The initial success of this program, borne out by the performance of the horses in races, has allowed for constant improvement of its installations, making it an important center of horse breeding and the main economic activity on the plantation today.

In the center of the reforested area two large ponds were built by damming up streams. In addition to enhancing the beauty of the natural environment they are excellent breeding grounds of fish and freshwater shrimp for both sport fishing and consumption. With a total area of four thousand acres, Juréa continues to be part of the jurisdiction of Dores do Piraí, today called Dorândia, even though the fazenda is directly linked to the municipal seat of Barra do Piraí, fifteen miles away.

PINHAL

To this day Pinhal retains its original furnishings and decor. The painting, by Benedito Calixto, depicts the fazenda in 1900.

Pinhal's history began precisely on December 30, 1785, when Carlos Bartolomeu de Arruda Botelho obtained a land grant "three leagues square" at the "stopping place" of Araraquara. The following year he received some neighboring lands as a gift, and in 1795 he enlarged his holdings even further with the purchase of the grant called Bom Jardim do Salto. His son Carlos José also received a grant, and the boundaries of both their properties, marked off in 1831, constituted the Pinhal grant. Its great house was built in 1830. Thereafter it underwent several enlargements and alterations, but its basic structure and appearance have always remained the same.

Carlos José and his brother Manuel Joaquim became prestigious plantation owners and fulfilled various public functions in Araraquara, displaying even then the affinity the Arruda Botelho family had for public service. When Carlos José died in 1854, the management of the family business fell to his son Antônio Carlos de Arruda Botelho, a merchant in Constituição, today the prosperous city of Piracicaba. In 1856 Pinhal officially became the property of Antônio Carlos. As business flourished, the São Joaquim and Santa Maria plantations were acquired and annexed to Pinhal; at the same time some of its lands were donated toward the establishment of the village of São Carlos and the construction of its church. These lands were designated municipal property in 1857, when others joined with the Arruda Botelhos to found the future town of São Carlos.

For a long time Pinhal's main source of income came from cattle raising on a large scale. Eventually, however, it switched to coffee, as so

OPPOSITE AND BELOW: *The great house at Pinhal is a valuable repository of São Paulo history. Modeled after the large, comfortable Portuguese urban houses of the eighteenth century, it retains the same simple, colonial charm it had when it was built in 1830. The photograph below was taken in 1909, just before the plantation switched from coffee to cotton.*

ABOVE: *A view of the garden from the house.*

ABOVE: *Antônio Carlos Arruda Botelho (1827–1901) and Ana Carolina de Melo Oliveira Arruda Botelho (1841–1945), Count and Countess of Pinhal. He, an outstanding citizen and planter, was noble not only by title but also by character. She was the beloved matriarch of the large Arruda Botelho family.*

OPPOSITE: *The beautiful chapel at Pinhal has been used by several generations of Arruda Botelhos for baptisms, marriages, and other religious rites.*

many São Paulo plantations did in the last decades of the century. In addition to managing the activities of the Pinhal plantation, Antônio Carlos devoted himself to business in Piracicaba. As a result of the political and administrative services he performed for the province of São Paulo, the imperial government awarded him the titles of baron in 1879, viscount in 1883, and, finally, count in 1887.

He was married in 1852 to Francisca Theodora Coelho, but she died soon thereafter, leaving him with a single young son. He was thirty-six when he was married a second time, to Ana Carolina de Melo Oliveira, from a Rio Claro family. No less than twelve children were born from that marriage. A prestigious figure and regional chief of the Liberal Party, Antônio Carlos was frequently visited at Pinhal by important people in provincial politics and administration.

With the shadow of abolition advancing, Antônio Carlos sought a substitute for slave labor. An experiment with Germans admitted under a sharecropping contract did not yield the expected results. Nevertheless, on December 31, 1887, the slaves who worked for the Count of Pinhal all received their certificates of emancipation. Although freed, few left the plantation, even after abolition the following year. The count died in the house at Pinhal in 1901, and his body was taken for burial to a cemetery in the city of São Paulo. In 1910 the plantation, under the management of his son, also Antônio Carlos, switched its activity to cotton planting, reducing coffee production.

A major renovation of the house took place in 1926. Another began in 1941 and took three years to complete. 1941 also marked the hundredth birthday of Ana Carolina, Countess of Pinhal. The event was celebrated by the entire Arruda Botelho family and became news throughout the country. The countess died four years later. In her will she requested her heirs to "do everything possible not to sell shares to outsiders, but to other heirs." That wish was fulfilled: not only have her descendants kept the plantation complex in family hands, but they also have maintained it in a good state of preservation to this day.

On the occasion of the centennial of the town of São Carlos homage was paid to its main founder, the Count of Pinhal, by erecting a statue of him on the square. The act took place in the presence of the president of the Republic, Juscelino Kubitschek, the governor of São Paulo, Jânio Quadros, and, representing the Brazilian imperial family, Prince Pedro Henrique of Orléans-Bragança.

In December 1981 the government of the state of São Paulo declared the house at Pinhal and its surroundings a historical landmark worthy of preservation. Although divested of the major part of its extensive lands, the great house at Pinhal remains, a serene witness to a beautiful history.

RESGATE

In spite of its resemblance to a two-story urban mansion, Resgate is in fact a one-story dwelling. Its lower level was originally a storage basement. The stone staircase leads to the main entrance.

OVERLEAF: *In striking contrast to the restraint of Resgate's exterior is the exuberance of its interior decor. In the dining room, for instance, the skillful, witty brush of Catalan artist José Maria Villaronga has transformed one wall into marble embellished by Corinthian columns, vases, and elaborate hangings.*

The municipality of Bananal is an area of São Paulo state that juts into the territory of the state of Rio de Janeiro; in 1854 it was the major coffee-producing region in all of Brazil. Two of its fazendas, Resgate and Bela Vista, were among the most important of the Empire. The magnificent interior decor of Resgate's great house is indicative of this status, and its importance has been recognized by the National Historical Heritage, which declared it a national landmark in 1969.

According to historian Nogueira Porto, "the name [Resgate] most likely had its origin in the buying of slaves who were already prisoners of tribal wars in Africa and therefore were *resgatados*, 'the ones ransomed' by Portuguese and Brazilian slave traders." In addition to coffee, Resgate produced most essentials, importing only items impossible to produce on its own land, such as salt and salted fish. It grew its own indigo, tobacco, raw sugar, and even cotton, from which coarse clothing for the slaves was woven, and it manufactured its own harnesses, horseshoes, ox carts, and furniture.

The estate was originally part of a land grant on the New Road awarded to Brás de Oliveira Arruda. Resgate's founder, Brigadier Inácio Cabral Monteiro de Barros, had married Oliveira Arruda's daughter, Alda Romano. The son of an important coffee planter, he began cultivation on the site in the early nineteenth century, just as the coffee cycle was becoming profitable and the groves of Rio were being extended to the fertile soil of Bananal.

About 1830 Brigadier Inácio sold the plantation to José de Aguiar Toledo, a native of the Azores who had settled in Bananal in 1770 and had established the São Francisco da Formiga fazenda on the banks of the Bananal River. He

and his wife, Maria Valim, would be the founders of a coffee-growing clan of great importance. On Toledo's death in 1838 one of his sons, Manuel de Aguiar Valim, inherited Resgate, described in the inventory as "a mile-and-a-half from east to west and three from north to south, a total of 3,600 acres." The same document also lists 153 slaves and 321,000 coffee trees.

Manuel de Aguiar Valim married the daughter of another wealthy planter, Comendador Luciano José de Almeida. Their seven children all married into the provincial and court aristocracy. One son, Luciano José de Almeida Valim, was granted the title Baron Almeida Valim. Another, Manuel, became Baron Aguiar Valim.

Manuel de Aguiar Valim ran the plantation for more than forty years, until his death in 1879. His accounts reveal the wealth typical of the time: 1,400,000 coffee trees, 662 slaves, Brazilian treasury bonds, letters of credit from the Bank of Brazil, United States bonds, bank accounts in London. Resgate was in effect the capital of an empire comprising both inherited lands and those absorbed through the purchase of four more plantations: Três Barras, Independência, Cruz, and Bocaina.

ABOVE: *The panels, bouquet, and paintings on this wall are all trompe l'oeil.*

OPPOSITE: *The little red berry brought happiness and wealth to Resgate, as this illusionistic panel in the dining room seems to suggest.*

By 1872 Bananal counted seventy coffee plantations and more than seven thousand slaves. Yet when the rail link between Rio and São Paulo was completed in 1877, the town was bypassed by the line, which followed the course of the Paraíba River. In reaction, Bananal's residents undertook the construction of a branch line to Rio. As the funds raised were inadequate for its completion, the owner of Resgate, the widow Domiciana de Aguiar Valim, made up the difference. Although the line no longer operates, the railroad station in Bananal still exists; built of iron sheeting imported from Belgium, its architecture is typical of the period.

The great house at Resgate probably dates to between 1840 and 1845. When the writer Augusto Emílio Zaluar visited Bananal in 1860, he observed that Manuel de Aguiar Valim's plantation was "famous not only as one of the best properties in the region but also for the good taste with which the rooms

OPPOSITE AND ABOVE: With its exquisitely painted and gilded walls and ceiling, and the delicate paintings of native birds on its door panels, Resgate's living room is one of the most splendid in Brazil.

are painted and for the chapel. . . . The paintings are from the skillful brush of José Maria Villaronga. The living room, all in white, with friezes and gilt decoration, has a very tasteful ceiling, and the delicate paintings on the door panels depict the best-known birds of Brazil, perched on their favored trees, the branches of which are heavy with delicious ripe fruit."

The acclaimed Catalan artist José Maria Villaronga has left a large collection of works throughout Rio and São Paulo. Active in Brazil by 1850, he had previously decorated the Church of the Holy Family in Tinguá. Villaronga was adept in the painting of allegorical motifs, flora, and landscapes, and expert in the trompe l'oeil style of his day.

In 1891, as the coffee cycle began to wane, Resgate was sold along with other properties, including the rail line, to the businessman Domingos Moutinho. His family lived there until the death of his son Fernando in 1912. Six years later it was purchased by the Uruguayan cattle rancher Pedro Velleda. In 1922 the firm of Barbosa & Albuquerque in the city of Rio de Janeiro took over the plantation, but it was soon acquired by Gustave Masset. In 1970 it was purchased by Carlos Eduardo Kramer Machado, who undertook the restoration of the property, which was already under the protection of the National Historical Heritage but in a pitiful state of disrepair.

After a long and painstaking restoration, Resgate came into the possession of its current owner, Carlos Henrique Ferreira Braga, who has taken great care to preserve its legacy. With a land area of 2,300 acres, it is located six miles from the city of Bananal. Where coffee once grew, cattle of the zebu breed Nelore and thoroughbred Arabian horses are now raised. As one of the few plantations supervised by the Heritage, the house has been opened to the public, who can now tour this historic residence.

VARGEM GRANDE

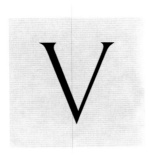

In creating the garden at Vargem Grande, landscape designer Roberto Burle Marx channeled the water that was formerly needed for coffee production into ornamental ponds and waterfalls.

Vargem Grande is situated only a few miles from the municipality of Areias, hemmed in by the high Bocaina Mountains. This region was the first in São Paulo to cultivate coffee in the early nineteenth century. The coffee groves of the São João Marcos region of Rio had already crossed the Coastal Range; soon they would penetrate the northern part of São Paulo, reaching the sites that were to become Areias, Bananal, Queluz, Silveiras, and São José do Barreiro—thriving towns that much later, as the coffee cycle declined, would inspire Monteiro Lobato's book *Dead Cities*, which recounts the death throes of the coffee-producing centers.

When Bavarian scientists Spix and Martius explored the region in 1819, they identified Areias as "a rather large settlement raised to the status of village by an act of King John VI in 1816," and noted that "many Indians live in the neighboring areas." The abundance of sand—*areia*—in local rivers and creeks may be the source of its name, although the historian Pedro Vallim traces "Areias" from the Indian word *aiê*, meaning "shortcut." In the 1820s, according to Afonso Taunay, plantation owners began building "the lordly residences that marked the high point of coffee civilization in São Paulo, before its movement to the western part of the province." By 1830, and for the next several decades, Areias and the neighboring town of Bananal were the leading producers of coffee in the province of São Paulo.

The New Road that first linked Rio de Janeiro and São Paulo provided easy access to Vargem Grande, which was established in 1834 by Otávio da Silva Leme. The great house, built the following year, is a one-story,

Located at the foot of the Bocaina Mountains, the simple, rather austere great house at Vargem Grande is modeled after a type of urban house common in the eighteenth century.

parallelogram-shaped structure over a "high," or "inhabitable," basement, the area used for storage of crops and other items. In style it resembles the eighteenth-century sugar-plantation houses of Minas Gerais. Vargem Grande distinguished itself as one of the most productive coffee plantations in the Paraíba valley of São Paulo. Generations of Lemes succeeded one another until 1888, when the emancipation of slaves hastened the decline of the coffee cycle. The consequent abandonment and decay of the coffee fazendas went on for many years, as can be seen in the sketches Tom Maia devoted to this region. As plantations were auctioned off to pay debts at the beginning of the twentieth century, Vargem Grande fell to José Assunção de Araújo, who tried in vain to revive the establishment. In 1928, with the construction of the highway between Rio de Janeiro and São Paulo, the hopes of some planters whose lands suddenly assumed new value were renewed. But at the end of the following year, the crash of the New York stock market had catastrophic consequences for Brazilian coffee, particularly for western São Paulo, whose major market was the United States.

The fazenda's former terreiro is now the site of Burle Marx's garden. The stone wall in the foreground was originally part of a system of dams and sluices necessary for coffee production.

A short time afterward, Vargem Grande was sold by the Araújos to the businessman Clemente Gomes. At that time he lived in São Paulo but had roots in and an affection for the countryside. Up until the 1960s the property maintained its activity, switching gradually from coffee growing to cattle raising, following the path of many fazendas in the state of Rio.

Beginning in 1970, Vargem Grande underwent a meticulous restoration that respected the house's original lines of construction. Renowned landscape designer Roberto Burle Marx restored the gardens. Vargem Grande was one of his last projects of this kind; one of the first was the garden of the São João sugar plantation in Pernambuco, restored in 1931 and also illustrated in this volume (see pages 176–83).

With the death of Clemente Gomes, the plantation went to his

LEFT: *Burle Marx transformed old objects found on the plantation into unique garden sculptures.*

BELOW: *Agaves thrive in the plantation's sandy soil.*

ABOVE: *The wide variety of trees and flowering plants offers a surprise at every turn of the garden's stone-paved paths.*

VARGEM GRANDE ∽ 129

ABOVE: *All the furnishings in the dining room are period pieces.*

OPPOSITE: *In the living room contemporary furniture shares space with a traditional cane rocking chair. The rug was also designed by the versatile Burle Marx.*

children and heirs, who, with dedication and good taste, have maintained its rustic grandeur. Its two thousand acres are utilized for reforestation and the raising of both beef and dairy cattle. The house itself has remained faithful to its original design, getting along without the alterations or "improvements" that so often accompany new wealth and modern conveniences. Vargem Grande retains its architectural integrity: simple but beautiful, it exudes the peace of a rural mansion.

São Martinho da Esperança

The former storage basement of the great house has been transformed into a reception area. The painting, only a small portion of which can be seen here, is by Guignard. It was recently purchased by Sérgio Sahione Fadel, the owner of Chacrinha (see pages 36–41).

A few miles from the city of Campinas and fifty-five miles from the capital of São Paulo lies one of the most important plantations in Brazil. The prosperous Campinas region and the São Paulo coffee cycle have given São Martinho da Esperança tradition and history. Beatriz Mendes Gonçalves Pimenta Camargo and Mário Pimenta Camargo, its owners, have given it soul and life.

Its proximity and easy access to São Paulo allow São Martinho da Esperança to fill an important role as a place for meetings, concerts, conferences, and weddings. People come from near and far: on a recent visit to Brazil, Margaret Thatcher was honored with a luncheon at São Martinho, satisfying her wish to see a Brazilian fazenda.

Toward the end of the eighteenth century, the land grant called Sete Quedas (Seven Falls), today Campinas, was awarded to Fernão Pompeu de Camargo. Its division among his children resulted in the creation of several plantations, two of which were particularly outstanding—Sete Quedas and Cachoeira, the latter being the early name of São Martinho da Esperança.

Cachoeira was founded by Antônio Pompeu de Camargo in 1823. Married to his cousin, Thereza Michelina do Amaral Pompeu, Antônio cleared forests and planted coffee trees on the virgin land, living in a modest dwelling prior to construction of the great house, which was begun about 1837 and finished in 1842.

The high moment for the property came when Francisco Emílio Amaral Pompeu received it as an inheritance. He had married the wealthy Gertrudes de Souza Aranha and had recourse to means adequate for the enrichment and

beautification of Cachoeira. In addition to expanding the coffee groves, the couple decorated the house with items that were unusual for São Paulo plantations. Of considerable artistic value, some of these treasures are renowned to this day, including a monumental brazier of gilded brass that is now in the collection of Isabel Cerquinho de Moraes Barros, and a silver tea and coffee service worthy of inclusion in the world's best collections. It belonged to Cecília Pompeu do Amaral Cunha Bueno and was recently acquired by Olavo Egídio Setúbal.

Francisco Emílio was succeeded by his son and heir, Raul Pompeu do Amaral. During his tenure Cachoeira continued attracting attention, its reputation for elegance and hospitality adhering not only to its owners but to their beautiful and esteemed daughter, Cecilinha da Cunha Bueno.

In 1945 the plantation was sold to Dario Freire Meirelles. He and his wife, Marieta Alves de Lima Meirelles, decided to transform the great house from a typical rural São Paulo dwelling of the nineteenth century into a palatial structure with monumental columns decorating the façade in a manner reminiscent of the plantation Tara in *Gone with the Wind.* The work, done by architect Jacques Pilon, did not detract from the original construction; rather, it lent the building a new distinction, as a comparison of the present house with an old sketch of it confirms (see page 17). At this time, too, the name was changed from Cachoeira to São Martinho.

This was a period when Brazilian industry was developing and replacing coffee in the export trade because new coffee-producing countries were entering the market, driving prices down. Plantations were forced to seek economic alternatives: Dario continued planting coffee of a new and less demanding variety, utilizing modern technology. São Martinho's importance, however, was as a model dairy farm. Not long after the establishment began raising Dutch cattle it gained fame throughout the country for the excellence of its organization. For a time, in the 1950s and 1960s, university-level courses in animal husbandry and related subjects were taught on the plantation.

In 1973 São Martinho was bought by the aforementioned Beatriz and Mário Pimenta Camargo. The story of their purchase has elements of a modern-day fairy tale. When they visited the house for the first time in 1957, they made a joint pledge: they would never be interested in any other rural property in São Paulo and they would wait for the moment when São Martinho could belong to them. That moment arrived in February 1973, when the Meirelles family sold them an option on the fazenda with the stipulation that if the court did not find in their favor, the Camargos would not receive their money back. Beatriz and Mário met with the court's approval and became owners of São Martinho, fulfilling against great odds their long-held hope; thus they added the "Esperança" to the name.

São Martinho da Esperança is enjoying a new and brilliant period. All manner of historical touches and modern conveniences have been added: drives have been paved with ancient stones; lampposts rescued from old towns in the interior of Bahia have been installed; luxuriant vegetation has been planted; and, above all, fine furniture and ornaments have been acquired, all selected with an eye to representing four centuries of Brazilian civilization. From the gold region and the Quebra-Canoa plantation, the owners have even brought an entire chapel painted by the outstanding master Manuel Ataíde in 1800.

The coffee groves have long since moved on from São Paulo to other regions. São Martinho da Esperança was one of the last plantations to surrender to the new reality: the fields, comprising 720 acres, are now planted with fodder, supporting a herd of zebu cattle of the Nelore breed. But the Camargos, in augmenting the beauty of the place, are careful to preserve its historic integrity, assuring future generations a knowledge of their past and its treasures.

ABOVE: *A former service building now functions as the pool house.*

LEFT: *Remodeled in the 1940s, São Martinho da Esperança now resembles the plantation houses of the American South.*

BELOW: *The large, multilevel terreiro is bordered on two sides by the fazenda's former granaries, as was customary on coffee plantations.*

EMPYREO

The last major addition to the great house at Empyreo was this veranda. Built along traditional lines, it is furnished with modern wicker pieces.

As the nineteenth century drew to a close, the province of Rio de Janeiro yielded its first-place status in coffee production to the province of São Paulo. Since the exporting of coffee was still the most important factor in the economy of the country in that pre-industrial era, São Paulo thus became absolutely vital to Brazil. It was a time of crisis in the coffee cycle, as the end of slavery coincided with the exhaustion of the land after decades of intense cultivation. São Paulo certainly suffered along with Rio, but the situation of the São Paulo growers was eased by concurrent developments in both labor and communications.

For some time the plantation owners had been replacing slave labor with free workers who had emigrated to Brazil from Europe, primarily from Italy. In 1867 the São Paulo Railway became operational, making the port of Santos accessible to the town of Jundiaí and from there to the coffee region by another rail line, the Paulista, famous for its high-quality service. The same period saw the construction of modern port facilities in Santos, making the handling of product more efficient and less costly. The Santos Dock Company obtained its concession toward the end of the Empire and put it to work during the first years of the Republic.

It was in the context of this favorable environment that Juvenal Penteado planned the construction of a house on his recently founded estate—"seed of the precious architectural relic that is the Empyreo plantation." It was to be a twentieth-century plantation, one of the largest and most important in coffee production during the São Paulo cycle.

RIGHT: *A family portrait and vintage photographs hang above a Dona Maria bed in one of the guest bedrooms.*

OPPOSITE: *As seen in this hallway, the interior decor of the house is a harmonious combination of period and modern furniture, chandeliers, and rugs.*

Its origins are shared with the Santo Antônio plantation in Araras, called by some its twin sister (see pages 148–53). Antônio Álvares de Almeida Lima, developer of the region, had acquired part of an estate known as Montevidéo. When that land was divided in 1863, several plantations were formed, including Empyreo. João Carlos Leite Penteado, the son-in-law of Antônio Álvares, and his wife, Maria Higina, had seven children. When João Carlos died in 1867, his widow married Joaquim Ferreira de Camargo Andrade, Baron of Ibitinga, who became administrator of Empyreo. In 1886 his stepson Juvenal Penteado took over the fazenda, and in 1892 he officially inherited it from his mother.

Juvenal was master of the plantation during the height of São Paulo's

coffee cycle: expanding his groves, he made the plantation a center of great wealth until his death in 1914. Guiomar, his widow and heiress, transferred half of Empyreo to their daughter Yolanda Penteado, who, buying the other half, became owner of the property. Yolanda's era is legendary. She was the wife for many years of Cicillo Matarazzo, a patron of the arts in Brazil and the founder of the São Paulo Museum of Art. In the 1940s and 1950s leaders in the world of letters, arts, and politics attended receptions at Empyreo, drawn by the prestige and warm hospitality of their hostess.

Located in the municipality of Leme, 125 miles from the state capital, São Paulo, the great house was built in three stages, with the first approximately a third of the size of the present building. The land is planted with thousands of coffee trees and a well-tended orange grove. Dairy cattle, hogs, sheep, and rabbits are bred and raised on the premises. About twenty years

OPPOSITE: *Empyreo's great house has tripled in size since the original structure was built in the mid-nineteenth century. The prosperity that coffee production brought to São Paulo well into the twentieth century made the additions to the house possible.*

RIGHT: *Graceful Louis-Philippe–style armchairs surround the long dining room table. Attractive lattice shutters diffuse bright sunlight without preventing fresh air from entering the room.*

OPPOSITE: *The chapel at Empyreo is a separate structure.*

RIGHT: *An eighteenth-century altar and a wooden santo, both from Bahia, are examples of the fazenda's notable art collection.*

ago the Penteado family transferred the property to Pedro Franco Piva, who continues the fine care this estate has enjoyed and maintains the tradition of hospitality. Empyreo has always been a pleasant retreat for its owners and visitors: marvelous works of art are displayed not only within the house but throughout the gardens as well. Piva continually embellishes the property with new acquisitions. In addition to valuable furniture and tapestries, the public rooms and bedrooms of the fazenda are decorated with the finest collections of china, porcelain, and crystal. Particularly notable is the collection of sculptures from the Brazilian northeast by the master Vitalino, as well as a distinctive collection of wooden images of saints.

SANTO ANTÔNIO

Lake Bartira, shrouded in the early morning mist, is bordered by an extensive lawn dotted with palm trees.

S anto Antônio is located in the Araras region of São Paulo, a locale that in 1818 was granted by the governor of São Paulo to Francisco Gois Maciel, Vicente Pires de Andrade, and Manuel da Rosa Maciel. The history of Araras officially began in July 1869, with the founding of the parish of Nossa Senhora do Patrocínio das Araras, which was raised to the status of a village two years later. It was finally made a municipality on January 7, 1873, and in April 1879 Araras was recognized as a town. From 1877 on, the municipal seat was served by the São Paulo Railway Company, to the great benefit of the regional economy. As discussed in the description of Santo Antônio's "twin sister" fazenda, Empyreo (see pages 140–47), the railway provided vital access to São Paulo and the important seaport of Santos, the main point of coffee exportation during the São Paulo cycle.

The plantation of Santo Antônio resulted from a transaction concluded on October 25, 1831, when Antônio Álvares de Almeida Lima acquired the site from Captain José Gonçalves Teixeira. At that time sugar cane cultivation dominated the region, but when coffee began to be grown in São Paulo, Santo Antônio soon became one of the largest producers. On the death of the founder in 1867 his two daughters, the future baronesses of Pirapitinguy and Ibitinga, inherited the plantation. Their husbands, already coffee barons, undertook the construction of the present-day seat between 1870 and 1875. They increased coffee production and made general improvements to the property. In the 1880s, during the course of the abolitionist movement, Italian settlers were contracted to substitute for slave labor, the availability

ABOVE: *Built in the 1870s, Santo Antônio's great house was designed by an Italian architect in the style of some southern Italian houses.*

OPPOSITE, TOP: *The second-story terrace overlooks Lake Bartira.*

OPPOSITE, BOTTOM: *This photograph of a Daimler-Benz with chauffeur and wolfhound in front of the house was taken in 1920, when the social and intellectual life at Santo Antônio was at its peak.*

of which was become scarcer and scarcer on large rural holdings. This proved to be the salvation of Santo Antônio, Empyreo, and the entire São Paulo coffee economy.

In 1892 the plantation became the property of Olívia Guedes Penteado and her husband, Ignácio Penteado, who were cousins (as well as grandchildren of Antônio Álvares). Ignácio was well qualified to administer Santo Antônio: he had been educated in England and was endowed with broad commercial acumen. Everything favored the third generation on the fazenda: the railroad, abundant inexpensive labor, a market at its height with the end of the Rio cycle, fertile red soil, and admirably flat topography. Ignácio and Olívia turned Santo Antônio into one of the most important coffee plantations in Brazil. They expanded their plantings prodigiously—the coffee groves consisted of more than two million trees, extraordinary for any period.

In this abundant era, the great house underwent many changes, including modernizations to fulfill new standards of comfort. Valuable pieces of furniture were acquired in Europe; the interior of Santo Antônio could be compared in its variety and quality to the most elegant rooms in the mansions of Rio and São Paulo. Sets of Adams and Mapple furniture bought in London would later share space with furniture from Olívia's Paris apartment. Along

with coffee production, cattle raising was developed; a factory for milk products was established, and it manufactured the first powdered milk in Brazil.

Ignácio Penteado died in 1915, and Olívia decided to turn over the administration of Santo Antônio to her daughter Carolina and her son-in-law Goffredo Teixeira da Silva Telles. During the 1920s the fazenda assumed a vibrant and varied life. In a short time the property was "populated" by Carolina and Goffredo's children, and the elegant mansion received the cream of Rio and São Paulo intellectuals, as well as international travelers of legendary status. Frequent visitors included the writers Blaise Cendrars, Oswald and Mário de Andrade, and Cassiano Ricardo; the Brazilian composer Heitor Villa-Lobos (famous for his adaptation of classical techniques to Afro-Brazilian themes); and Lasar Segall, Anita Malfati, and Tarsila do Amaral, artists of growing reputation in North as well as South America.

The disastrous repercussions that the crash of the New York stock market had on Brazilian coffee exports was aggravated by a crisis of overproduction—a surplus of coffee along with a drop in price—resulting in widespread burning of excess stores, a policy that would ruin many planters.

ABOVE: *The main staircase features carved wooden balusters of an elegant design.*

OPPOSITE: *High-arched openings between rooms, typical of nineteenth-century Brazilian architecture, aid ventilation.*

In 1931, in the midst of this difficult period, Santo Antônio was officially turned over to Carolina and Goffredo Telles. Starting in 1935, as the impracticality of a coffee monoculture was becoming evident, the cattle-raising operation was intensified and Santo Antônio went back to growing sugar cane for its mills. During this phase one of the couple's sons, Gilberto Silva Telles, actively participated in the economic revamping of the plantation. In the 1970s one of their daughters, Maria Eugênia, was put in charge.

Before Goffredo's death in 1980 the couple decided to divide the 8,500-acre fazenda into seven parts— one for each child—maintaining, however, the magnificent seat and the surrounding 150 acres as a common area to be shared by all, with Carolina as its usufructuary. Carolina celebrated her hundredth birthday in 1994.

Although it has been reduced in size and is no longer an active producer, Santo Antônio retains its unique atmosphere and impressive sense of scale, sustained by the lore of the Telles family. Through consecutive generations, family members have faithfully preserved the heart of the fazenda. Installations from previous periods are in a fine state of conservation, as is the forest preserve and the beautiful pond created by Antônio Álvares. The seat, covering an acre and a half, has had some alterations. The interior decor is eclectic, with nineteenth-century furniture alongside pieces of other periods and styles. It is worth mentioning certain parts of the complex: the administration building, built in 1845; the well-cared-for garden with an outstanding rose arbor; the modern swimming pool with bathhouses; the orchard with various kinds of fruit trees; the storage bins from the coffee era; the former slave quarters; the sawmill, an ancient installation imported from England; the building from "New Holland," which houses the milk industry; the coach house with a few remaining specimens; a spacious barn for two hundred dairy cows; and a functioning school.

SANTA GERTRUDES/ PARAGUASSU

D uring the first half of the nineteenth century São Paulo was not immune to the coffee boom that transformed the province of Rio de Janeiro. Even then groves were beginning to spread into the region of São Paulo where they are found today, notably the forward-looking towns of Campinas and Rio Claro.

A charming turn-of-the-century belvedere affords a sweeping view of the surrounding countryside.

It was on the Ibiacaba fazenda in nearby Limeira that Nicolau Pereira de Campos Vergueiro—a senator, minister, and imperial counselor—first recruited European immigrants as workers. They would come to replace slave labor, which was at that time predominant on plantations in the Paraíba do Sul River valley.

In viewing the fazendas of São Paulo, one cannot fail to be continually reminded that when coffee arrived in this area by way of Areias and Bananal, it brought with it the greatest agricultural wealth that São Paulo has known. For the red earth of São Paulo was rich. Even before the opening of railways in the center of the province, beginning in 1867 with the linking of the port of Santos to the town of Jundiaí, São Paulo coffee groves were already competitive with those of neighboring Rio townships.

In the 1840s Galvão de França and Barros Ferraz sold some of their land, which had been part of the legendary Morro Azul grant. The buyers were Gertrudes Galvão de Oliveira Lacerda and her husband, Brigadier Manuel Rodrigues Jordão, the parents of Amador Rodrigues de Lacerda Jordão, Baron of São João do Rio Claro.

On this land, famous for the quality of its soil, the Jordãos founded four important plantations: Morro Azul, Paraguassu, Laranja Azeda or Santa

ABOVE: *One of the many* terreiros *at Santa Gertrudes is bordered by the machine shop, where coffee beans were weighed and bagged.*

RIGHT: *Cane fields have replaced coffee groves on the fazenda. Here sugar cane is ready to be harvested.*

Gertrudes, and Ibiacaba, the model fazenda where free immigrant laborers were first employed.

Santa Gertrudes was named for Gertrudes Galvão; she and her husband were renowned for their great wealth and political prestige. When Emperor Pedro II and Empress Tereza Cristina visited São Paulo in February 1846, the emperor traveled into the interior, while the empress stayed for almost two months at Gertrudes's city mansion on the Largo do Braz. On the eve of the imperial couple's departure, Gertrudes gave a splendid ball in their honor.

The Baron of São João do Rio Claro inherited the Santa Gertrudes plantation upon his parents' death. A deputy from São Paulo for several terms, he was married to Maria Hipólita, daughter of Joaquim José dos Santos Silva, Baron of Itapetininga. When Rio Claro died in 1873, Maria Hipólita married again. Her new husband was Joaquim Egídio de Sousa Aranha, Baron, Viscount, Count, and Marquis of Três Rios, whose fortune at the time was considered one of the greatest in São Paulo.

Tracks connect the upper story of the machine shop with the terreiro.

Surviving Três Rios and having no descendants, on her death in 1894 Maria Hipólita bequeathed Santa Gertrudes to her half-sister, Antônia Joaquina, married to Count Eduardo Prates by pontifical concession. It is curious to note that Antônia Joaquina was the daughter of Cirina Joaquina, whose first husband had been the Baron of Itapetininga; her second was Francisco Xavier Pais de Barros, Baron of Tatui. She lived on her estate, the Chácara do Chá, right in the heart of the city of São Paulo, where today the Chá viaduct is located.

It was during Eduardo Prates's tenure that Santa Gertrudes enjoyed its most brilliant phase, just as São Paulo coffee came into its own out of the ashes of the Rio cycle. Assuming direction of the São Paulo Railway Company and administration of the plantation, Prates gave new impetus to the old property. He increased the growing area with the acquisition of new lands; built large terraces for drying the coffee beans in the sun; installed modern equipment; built dozens of outbuildings and houses for workers; erected a new and luxurious seat, furnished for comfort and with space for all necessary operations; restored the old 1866 chapel (at the same time transforming it into a genuine private church); and planted a beautiful garden surrounded by a reservoir. All of these augmentations were fitting to Santa Gertrudes, now a coffee-growing establishment whose importance rose with that of the São Paulo coffee cycle.

Prates's son Guilherme dos Santos Prates succeeded his father as owner and as the dedicated administrator of the plantation. During this phase Santa Gertrudes consisted of slightly more than six thousand acres. After Guilherme's

ABOVE: *Even though Santa Gertrudes abandoned coffee production years ago, its great house still stands at the center of the fazenda's coffee-growing complex; nothing was torn down, replaced, or changed. As a living museum, it evokes an era that will never return.*

OPPOSITE: *Facing the great house across the terreiro is the fazenda's church, restored in 1898. Whether because of its architectural beauty or because of the prestige that the plantation and Count Prates enjoyed, the Vatican itself took note of the church.*

death the property was divided up equally among his three daughters. One of them, Maria Cândida Prates Baeta Neves, widow of Luís Felipe Baeta Neves, received the seat, all the improvements, 1,800 acres, and the liabilities of the plantation.

Paraguassu, a neighboring plantation and today an integral part of the Santa Gertrudes complex, also originally belonged to the wealthy Jordãos who had purchased the Morro Azul lands in the 1840s. But it was the Almeida Prado family from Jaú who founded the Paraguassu plantation and managed it for three generations. The seat, today altered by additions, was built in the middle of the nineteenth century. Acquired by Maria Cândida's father-in-law, the physician Luís Felipe Baeta Neves, it was passed on to his son, an engineer of the same name.

Maria Cândida lives at Santa Gertrudes with a lady companion and servants. Maria Candinha, her daughter and heir, lives at Paraguassu with her husband, José Honorato Gago da Câmara Botelho de Medeiros, son of the third Viscount of Botelho in Portugal, owner of the traditional Monte Simplício estate on the island of São Miguel.

Both plantations presently grow sugar cane for the production of fuel alcohol. A new Luís Felipe, son of José Honorato and Maria Candinha, is a recently graduated agronomist and represents the new generation that is assuming the administration of the plantations, which have witnessed so much change and so much continuity.

SANTA CLARA

The rear façade of the great house at
Santa Clara is built in the chalet style.

T he Santa Clara fazenda possessed two seats—both still in
existence and well preserved. What usually happened when
coffee plantations became prosperous was that either the original
residence was remodeled and enlarged, or a new house, larger
and grander, was built to replace the old one. The early houses were,
naturally, modest dwellings, built in no particular architectural style and of
a size dictated purely by the necessities of family life. As time went by and
the profits came rolling in—quick, fantastic profits on an order completely
unanticipated—the new money brought about a radical change in the habits
and customs of those caught up in the coffee whirlwind. Suddenly there
was interest in higher education, trips to the provincial capital and to the
imperial court itself, and attendance at parties, the theater, concerts. In
some cases there was a craving for entry into politics, exercise of position,
closeness to power. Titles of nobility were forthcoming, forming the
framework of an aristocratic society that was consolidated and shaped by
wealth. It was, in short, a new way of life, luxurious and ostentatious.

At just such a moment the original seat of Santa Clara was abandoned
and a new one built near the first. In this case, quite unusually, the old house
was preserved. The grander house displays French architectural influences.
It is laid out in the shape of a T, the broad part of which is occupied by an
enormous dining room. This largest of scale is not evident from the front,
however, which gives the impression of more modest dimensions. The
construction shows refinement in its finishings, with abundant use of Riga
pine and decorative elements whose eccentric cast reflects the ambience at

the end of the coffee cycle. High-relief decoration of doors and windows provides a certain delicacy, a sense of care. Elegantly arched windows with colored panes lend brilliance and grace to the house.

Located in Minas Gerais in the Kágado Pequeno River valley, part of the Paraíba basin, Santa Clara belongs to the Sossego district of the municipality of Santana do Deserto, which in times past was part of the city of Juiz de Fora. The *Album of the Municipality of Juiz de Fora*, published in 1915, claimed that this fazenda was the first in the region and that the Cachoeira and Serra plantations belonged to the same owner.

In his memoir *Trunk of Bones*, the writer Pedro Nava, considered by many to be the Brazilian Proust, refers to the "pastoral symphony of the fazenda Santa Clara," so impressed was he by the songs of the birds. Nava recalls spending time there with his family in 1903, when he was a child convalescing from an illness. From his narrative it can be established that the owner of the plantation was Manuel da Silva Carneiro, who at that time was celebrating the twenty-fifth anniversary of his purchase of Santa Clara from the former owner, Pedro de Alcântara Cerqueira Leite, Baron of São João Nepomuceno, an event that can therefore be dated to 1878, at the height of

OPPOSITE: *The front façade is, in the words of architect Alcides Miranda, "gracefully neoclassical," whereas the wider part, in the rear, "is composed of a grouping of chalets."*

BELOW: *The stables are of recent construction.*

ABOVE: *The rudimentary copper equipment for producing cachaça is still in use today.*

OPPOSITE: *The large main dining room, elegantly appointed with nineteenth-century jacaranda furniture, runs the width of the rear part of the house.*

the coffee cycle. Nava notes that Manuel Carneiro was "an intimate friend of my grandfather, and godfather at my mother's wedding." As for the house, he records the impressions that remained with him: "Mr. Carneiro's house didn't look at all like the other fazendas in the region. It was like a city residence, full of porcelain, silver, linens, and table services. All white and square . . . doors and windows displayed decorated frames, with a central pane of sapphire blue. Parlors in the front, a hallway with innumerable bedrooms. . . ." He goes on to describe the house as being surrounded by gardens and recalls a shed for storage of corn, terraces for drying, a dam for the breeding of carp and prawns, and an orchard where the most appreciated native and European fruits could be picked.

Eight miles from the municipal seat, Santa Clara belonged to the heirs of the Carneiro family until it was acquired by Mauro Campos in the 1980s. Today it is undergoing a rejuvenation as careful restoration work proceeds and the collection of furniture and decorative objects is repaired and augmented. The revamped decor and furniture now reflect the orientation of Arnaldo Danemberg, antiquarian and scholar of Luso-Brazilian furniture. The architect Gabriela Machado is also involved in the work. The conservation and refurbishment conciliate modern comforts with faithfulness to the original heritage and style. The gardens of Santa Clara, with royal palms as witnesses, evoke Pedro Nava's exact memories. With an area of four thousand acres, the plantation's fields support a herd of zebu cattle of the Guzerat breed and three hundred thoroughbred Mangalarga riding horses.

BARRA DO PEIXE

I n 1780, by an act of the governor of the captaincy of Minas Gerais, Luís da Cunha Menezes, "Porto Novo do Cunha" became the name of a new municipality on the banks of the Paraíba do Sul River. Today it is called Além Paraíba. It was here, on the left bank of the wide Paraíba, that Comendador Simplício José Ferreira da Fonseca founded the Barra do Peixe plantation in 1859, during the heyday of the coffee cycle. Located in the district previously known as Conceição and in 1871 renamed Simplício in honor of the comendador, Barra do Peixe derived its name from the Peixe River, which crosses through it, forming a handsome waterfall with multiple cataracts precisely at the point where it passes the great house.

The founder of the plantation was a man of resolve, intelligence, and culture, esteemed by all who knew him. Along with his cousin, the great entrepreneur Mariano Procópio Ferreira Lage, Simplício had been active in the construction of the Union and Industry Highway, the most important highway project of the Second Empire. Inaugurated on June 23, 1861, by Emperor Pedro II, it linked Petrópolis, close to the imperial court at Rio, with Juiz de Fora, an important city in Minas Gerais.

In the process of building the road, Simplício was in charge of two thousand carts along with their teams, as well as a large number of laborers. With equal dedication he took part in the construction of the railroad when tracks were laid to Porto Novo in 1871. Having an administrator of that caliber, the Barra do Peixe plantation was destined to become an important and prosperous rural establishment.

In travel impressions published in 1941, an American named Herbert H. Smith refers to the "great plantation of Mr. S.," which he defines as "a small world." Without giving the owner's full name, Smith reports that the mysterious "Mr. S" had visited several countries in Europe and on his return tried to apply to his plantation the latest agricultural methods that he had observed in use on the Continent.

Also to the credit of the founder of Barra do Peixe was the donation of buildings on his property for the establishment of a mayor's office, chamber, court, and school when the municipality of São José de Além Paraíba was

founded. Unfortunately, all of these structures have been torn down or are in a deteriorated state today. There is even more to lament. At his own expense, Simplício built a beautiful church dedicated to Our Lady of Bethlehem on plantation land, near the station that bore its name. Donated to the local diocese, it ended up being demolished after a long period of abandonment.

Married three times, the comendador observed the custom of giving a plantation to each of his children upon marriage, a practice common during the golden age of coffee. Thus the Conceição, Gironda, Simplício, and neighboring Santa Alda plantations passed into the hands of his offspring. The great house at Santa Alda, built for son-in-law Teixeira Soares, became renowned for its generous dimensions.

After Simplício's death in 1894, Barra do Peixe was sold and resold more than once and went into accelerated decline. In 1976, in a precarious state of preservation, it was bought by Cândida and Joaquim Guilherme da Silveira, who have devotedly restored the whole plantation complex, beginning with the mansion and its seventeen windows. So beautiful and appreciated was the work that when it was finished it merited a long, illustrated article in the *New York Times* of May 19, 1983, with the title "Plantation House in Brazil Regains Its Former Glory." In the article, Cândida Silveira explains how Barra do Peixe met her three wishes in the choice of a plantation: it was an old house, it was on a hill, and there was a waterfall nearby. The house has been appointed with fine Brazilian furniture from the eighteenth and

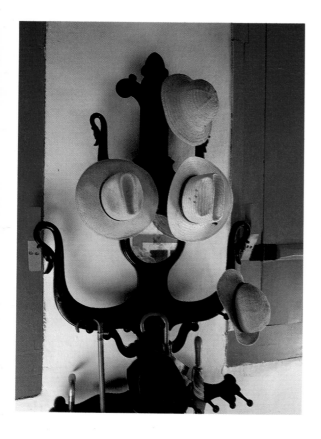

ABOVE: *This whimsically shaped hat rack has arms in the form of swans.*

RIGHT: *A soothing landscape is painted on the headboard of this bed.*

OPPOSITE: *The windows in all of the bedrooms are fitted with sturdy wooden shutters operated by a traditional iron mechanism.*

OVERLEAF: *The great house at Barra do Peixe was built during the first years of the coffee cycle in Minas Gerais and has retained the unadorned beauty of its original design.*

nineteenth centuries, in addition to the most varied decorative pieces of diverse origins. Sweeping lawns, beds of blooming flowers, and ponds complete the residential environment.

Consisting of 3,600 acres, the productive sector of the plantation also received the Silveiras' attention with the establishment of a breeding program of Indian beef cattle of the Nelore breed. On a much smaller scale, a herd of dairy cows fills the needs of the plantation, and what is left over is sold. The fazenda grows its own subsistence crops, and an important forest reserve is also maintained.

SÃO JOÃO

Each end of São João's front façade culminates in a graceful round veranda. This one is furnished with modern wicker armchairs.

F or hundreds of years, endless fields of sugar cane were cultivated in the region known as the Water Plains of Pernambuco, bordering the Capibaribe River on the outskirts of Recife. The first plantings date to the early sixteenth century, a time just after Brazil had been discovered and when the hereditary captaincy of Duarte Coelho—grantee of Pernambuco—was at its peak. It is in this fabled land that we find the great house of the São João *engenho*, or sugar plantation. Although the house itself is of relatively recent construction, the property was witness to the Dutch invasion of the seventeenth century and is among the oldest in Pernambuco.

The beginning of the Portuguese colonial period in Brazil centered on the planting of cane and the exporting of dyewood. The most important plantations of Pernambuco were located close to the site where the early settlement of Recife was founded. With the Dutch invasion of 1630, most of the rural properties of the vicinity were abandoned by their terrified owners, who fled to escape the sacking and burning of their plantations; at times fires were set by the colonizers themselves to deny the spoils of war to the invaders. Some, however, pressed by their dependents and seeing no alternative, capitulated to the new realities and collaborated with the Dutch, thus preserving their estates.

Such was the case of the Portuguese João Fernandes Vieira, a native of the island of Madeira. Ambitious and skilled, he resolved to maintain good relations with the Dutch authorities and merchants. Quickly winning their trust, and even going into partnership with enemy merchants, he soon managed to recover his properties. In 1642, during the truce between Portugal and Holland, he received a loan from the Dutch West Indies Company to finance the cultivation of his plantations. In the attendant document, Vieira lists as his plantations Santo Antônio, São João, São Carlos or Meio, Sant'Ana, and Ilhetas. By the very number of plantations one can assume that the fortune of the master of São João was considerable. In the same document he agreed to turn over his entire production to the company.

Before being called São João, the plantation was known as Nossa Senhora do Rosário and, evolving with the improvement of sugar manufacture, went from employing primitive grinders to the use of water mills. The new name may have referred to the owner's religious devotion to Saint John the Baptist, or it may instead have implied a political "devotion" to King John IV, the first sovereign following the Restoration of 1640, when Portugal freed itself from Spanish domination.

In 1645 the so-called Pernambucan Insurrection broke out. It was an armed movement destined finally to expel the Dutch invaders from Brazilian soil. History records the military plans for the rebellion as having been discussed and approved at São João. João Fernandes Vieira commanded the insurrection. Joined by André Vidal de Negreiros, Henrique Dias, and Felipe Camarão—all famous names in seventeenth-century Brazilian history—he led hundreds of colonists, blacks, and Indians to victory.

In 1660 Portugal and Holland signed a peace treaty, in which the former invader demanded heavy redress for properties abandoned in Brazil, including the plantations it had taken over. João Vieira vehemently opposed the Dutch demands in his will of 1673. After listing the properties he owned, including São João, he comments ironically that "he owes nothing to the Dutch, who should first restore to him, the deponent, the fine dinners he gave them for eight or nine years." He then goes on to enumerate damages suffered during the foreign occupation.

Following the dominion of Vieira, there is no mention of subsequent owners of the sugar establishment during the colonial period.

In the twilight phase of the sugar cycle, São João survived as a sugar producer in the modified role of a factory processing cane grown elsewhere. In 1894 the owner was Francisco do Rego Barros Lacerda, who willed it to his heirs. The industrial mill was serviced by a twenty-four-mile railway, with rails of one-meter gauge. Taking the place of the ancient slave quarters was a workers' village of seventy houses, complete with medical and social services.

At the end of the nineteenth century an imposing seat was built on the site of the old São João plantation, a work undertaken by the industrialist Ricardo Lacerda de Almeida

OPPOSITE: *Decorated entirely with Manueline-style furniture, the dining room has a stately air.*

BELOW: *An intricately carved and inlaid wood and ivory cabinet of Japanese origin has pride of place in the so-called Japanese parlor.*

OPPOSITE: *A collection of rare eighteenth-century Portuguese and Brazilian plates adorns the dining room walls. The cane-backed chairs and sofa are of nineteenth-century Brazilian manufacture.*

BELOW: *This flower arrangement, designed by Roberto Burle Marx shortly before his death, is his expression of "the best of Brazil."*

BELOW: *The use of iron became widespread in Brazil in the last quarter of the nineteenth century. Prefabricated iron houses, sheds, and bridges were imported and assembled on arrival. The great house at São João, known as the House of Iron, is a rare example of an opulent residence built during the twilight of the sugar cycle, and one of the country's finest examples of the use of iron for domestic architecture.*

Brennand. The structural framework, inside and out, is of cast iron, imported for the most part from Belgium, and the place came to be known as the House of Iron. This material was broadly used in residential construction during the second half of the nineteenth century, particularly for urban dwellings. In imperial Brazil whole structures of cast iron were imported and used in a wide range of construction projects, from highway and railway bridges to railroad stations; many of these structures are still standing. Another example is the unique metal-and-glass Crystal Palace, built in 1884 as an exhibition hall for

OPPOSITE: *An elaborately ornamented, X-shaped iron staircase dominates the interior courtyard.*

flower shows in Petrópolis, the imperial city that is now a summer resort for residents of Rio.

São João long ago abandoned the cane fields that once covered several districts of what is now Recife, the capital of Pernambuco. Located in the Várzea district, a few miles from the center, the House of Iron stands today as an extraordinary period structure. Marvelously well preserved, it is still in the Brennand family, being the residence of owner Cornélio Brennand. São João is now the site of various industrial activities, among them the manufacture of tiles and other ceramics. In the 1930s landscape designer Roberto Burle Marx, at that time a resident of Recife and at the beginning of establishing his international reputation, designed the gardens that still surround the house.

FREGUESIA

The great house of the Freguesia sugar plantation is one of the oldest and most expressive rural residences in Brazil. It can be found on the shore of the Bahia de Todos os Santos, the Bay of All Saints, forty-five miles from Salvador, in the town of Candeias. Although somewhat transformed by successive remodelings, it is, remarkably, the original structure, whose thick walls have stood up to the centuries and borne witness to the entire evolution of the sugar cycle.

Most eighteenth-century sugar-plantation houses were built in a simple, unadorned style known as Luso-Brazilian. Freguesia, with its majestic chapel, however, was an exception to the rule. It bears the marked influence of the Portuguese baroque, which was used in Brazil only for structures of great importance.

Freguesia appears on the very oldest maps of Bahia, made during the century of the discovery of Brazil, along with two other plantations annexed to it, Caboto and Matoim, both presently in ruins. Its remote origins have their beginning in a land grant of 1560, whose beneficiary was the Portuguese Sebastião Alves. Its founding coincides with the establishment of the sugar industry in Bahia, when the general government of the colony was set up there. Twenty-four years later the property passed to Sebastião Faria, Sebastião Alves's son. In its first form the vast holding drew the attention of Gabriel Soares de Souza, a chronicler of the colonial period, who mentioned it in his *Descriptive Treatise on Brazil* of 1587, stressing the "big buildings of the mill, refinery, living quarters, and workshops."

From 1624 to 1625, during the Dutch occupation of Salvador, then the capital of Brazil, the invaders burned Freguesia and the adjoining Church of Our Lady of Mercy. Even after being driven out, they would return in isolated raids that resulted in the destruction of twenty-seven cane-grinding establishments and the loss of many lives in a war without quarter.

OPPOSITE: *A cradle of French origin and an Empire-style bed are exhibited in this bedroom. Donated by the Wanderley Pinho family, the last owners of the plantation, all the furnishings now on display belonged to the house in the past.*

ABOVE: *This canopy bed is in the Dona Maria style.*

LEFT: *The only remaining indications of the once sumptuously decorated reception room are a few pieces of furniture and the coat of arms of the Count of Passé, still emblazoned on the ceiling.*

In the 1680s Antônio da Rocha Pita acquired the property, which, properly restored, would in 1760 pass on to his grandson, Captain-Major Cristóvão da Rocha Pita. Wanderley Pinho, author of *History of a Plantation on the Bay,* a book on Freguesia, presumes that the grandson was responsible for the construction of the present-day great house, which can be dated with certainty to the eighteenth century. Influenced by Portuguese baroque, it has the look of a palace. Among the outstanding members of the family who owned the plantation in the eighteenth century was Sebastião da Rocha Pita, author of *History of Portuguese America,* published in Portugal in 1730. Set on high, the great house, served by a dock, enjoys a splendid view of the sea and the famous island of Maré, which was celebrated by the colonial poet Manuel Botelho de Oliveira. The building consists of four stories that preserve structural elements dating from the eighteenth century, although the grillwork on the balconies was added in renovations of the following century.

In 1848 Antônio Bernardino da Rocha Pita Argolo, who would receive the title Count of Passé, acquired the group of sugar installations, which he left on his death in 1877 to his granddaughters Maria Luisa and Antônia Teresa, the daughters of João Maurício Wanderley, Baron of Cotegipe. A prestigious politician of the Second Empire, the baron took over the administration of the plantation. With the marriage of João Ferreira de Araújo Pinho to the first of the heiresses, the property passed into the hands of the newlyweds. Araújo Pinho, from a traditional Bahian family, went on to be governor of the State of Bahia from 1908 to 1912.

The Count of Passé's great-grandson Wanderley Pinho wrote of him: "With work, diligence, and ability, as well as the gifts and inheritances that came his way, he would amass the greatest fortune of his time and one of the greatest of all time in Bahia." On the occasion of the Campaign for Independence in that province, the Count of Passé joined the so-called Liberating Army, and during the period of the Regencies he took part in the resistance against the rebel movement known as the Sabinada. On the ceiling of one of the salons of Freguesia his coat of arms figures prominently.

The owners of the plantation always tried to keep up with the latest technology in sugar production. By 1850 the primitive capstans that were moved by animals to turn the grinding stones had already been replaced by steam engines. To set this advance in context: in 1833, on the province's 603 registered sugar plantations, 46 of the mills were powered by steam engine, 62 by waterwheel, and 495 by animal power.

In 1900 Freguesia stopped grinding cane, leaving that operation to neighboring properties. It was the foreshadowing of an irreversible decline. The National Historical Heritage took over the property on September 14, 1944. It was then expropriated by the state government in January 1968

The Bay of All Saints, as seen from the shore opposite the plantation. Proximity to water, whether sea or river, was essential to sugar plantations for facilitating the transportation of the sugar produced by their mills.

and transformed into the Wanderley Pinho Museum of the Bay. Two years later restoration of all the buildings began, under the direction of architects from the Historical Heritage. The institution was opened to the public in 1971.

The only extant sugar plantation in Bahia that preserves house, chapel, and mill, it also features a collection of equipment used during the various periods of sugar production in the bay area. Examples of the original furnishings of the house are on exhibit in the mansion, as are religious artifacts from the Church of Our Lady of Mercy of Matoim, including its ancient baptismal font and images of Our Lady of Mercy, Saint Jerome, and Saint John.

A stroll through Freguesia's parlors, bedrooms, alcoves, and hallways arouses a pleasant sensation of returning to bygone days, to a slow and intense way of life. As a museum, Freguesia shelters, recalls, and keeps alive for future generations the memories of an influential chapter in the economic and social history of Brazil.

GRUTA

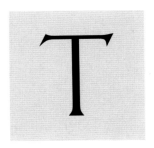

When open, these attractive doors provide a view of the southern plains, where Devon cattle graze.

The vast expanse of Gruta is located in the state of Rio Grande do Sul, twenty-four miles from Pelotas, which in the nineteenth century was the most prosperous town in the province. A quintessential *estância*, or cattle ranch, Gruta experienced all phases of Rio Grande development. Many years ago, its 25,000 acres of grazing land supported an excellent herd of Devon cattle, a breed originating in England. They arrived there through the English breeder French, owner of a ranch in Uruguay, who in 1915 sold his complete stock to Rio Grande do Sul. Half went to Gruta, then owned by Edmundo Berchon des Essarts, and half to Pedras Altas, the famous estância of Francisco Assis Brasil. A diplomat and resident of England for many years, Assis Brasil was also an experienced cattle breeder. He judged the pastures and climatic conditions of Rio Grande do Sul to be similar to those of the county of Devon, and felt that the Devon breed should do well there. Assis and his good friend Berchon were right: still importing breeding stock from England, in 1942 the Gruta ranch had the largest purebred herd in the world.

The history of Gruta's fields began with a grant by the Portuguese Crown in 1777 to Sergeant-Major Roberto Roiz. The territory where the ranch would arise was situated between the Contrabandista and Piratini rivers. Domingos de Castro Antiquera, who would be named Baron and later Viscount of Jaguari, married one of Roiz's daughters and succeeded him on the grant. Their daughter Clara Joaquina and her husband, Antônio Soares de Paiva Filho, were the parents of Bernardina Soares de Paiva, who in 1853 built the central house at Gruta, which looks just the same today.

ABOVE: *The modest chapel is a poignant reminder of the past.*

OPPOSITE: *A family portrait hangs above nineteenth-century furniture in the entrance hall.*

At that time the ranch itself was small. The fields belonged to Antônio José Gonçalves Chaves, who had bought them from the grandchildren of Roberto Roiz. Gonçalves Chaves was a man ahead of his time. A wealthy producer of dried beef, he was host to Auguste Saint-Hilaire, who would describe him as having a good command of both French and Latin and a broad knowledge of natural history. Saint-Hilaire recalled the Chaves home as being situated beside the Pelotas River and flanked by a broad field on one side and numerous racks for hanging salted meat on the other.

Edmundo Berchon des Essarts slowly acquired lands from the heirs of Gonçalves Chaves. When he finally bought the seat of Gruta, by then the property of Bernardina's daughter Maria Pinto, he put together his great ranch. The first generation of the Essarts would go on to write the most important phase of the estância's history.

The name of the town of Pelotas means "balls," referring to rolls of cowhide that had been specially processed for sale. This name recalls the long period when cattle were butchered for hides alone. The situation was changed by the innovation of jerked beef—the transformation of raw meat into dried beef. Developed as a means of saving waste products, the dried beef came to enrich those who produced it, leading to the growth of Pelotas in the nineteenth century.

The second generation of Berchons on the Gruta ranch was led by Vera des Essarts Carvalho, Edmundo's daughter, who married the physician Jaime de Carvalho. The ranch then passed to her daughter, Antônia de Oliveira Sampaio, who, along with her daughters, Maria Rita, Rosa May, and Anna Luiza, formed the family's third and fourth generations. They managed their inheritance with great care and dedication.

Antoninha Berchon, as Antônia Sampaio was known, was no ordinary person. A glowing affability suffused her personality, making her a magnetic force held in high esteem in her southern community as well as in Rio de

RIGHT: *The fireplace is permanently lit to boil the water for maté, the caffeine-rich drink that is a staple on estâncias. Since everyone drinks it out of the same receptacle—a gourd—the custom promotes friendly companionship.*

OPPOSITE: *This multiple-use building houses a stable, storeroom, and garage. The tower in the center recalls the defense towers that were erected in the days of border disputes, but it is in fact a water tank.*

BELOW: *Ranch hands, protected from the cold by their ponchos, leave at dawn for another workday. The lassoes tied to their saddles and the dogs running alongside the horses will help them herd the cattle.*

Janeiro, where she lived for many years. In addition to supervising the Gruta ranch, her permanent residence, Antoninha was also dedicated to the restoration and preservation of the historical heritage of Pelotas. Evoking the golden age of the city is the Municipal Park Museum of the Baroness, located in the splendid neoclassical house of Aníbal Antunes Maciel and Amélia Hartley de Brito, Baron and Baroness of Três Serras, who received it in 1864 as a wedding present. Another historical monument in the town is the theater, built in 1834 and still fully functional today. Finally, mention must be made of the Commercial Club of 1881, housed in a luxurious mansion that had once served as the residence of a wealthy meat producer.

In addition to the breeding of Devon cattle, a principal activity of the Gruta ranch is the breeding of sheep and horses. In agriculture, rice fields have been developed, and new techniques of pasturing are being tried, in order to find the best quality and greatest return.

Most recently, Gruta has been preparing to establish a program for cross-breeding Devon cattle with the American Litman breed. Unlike sugar and coffee plantations, which saw their furnaces turned off and coffee groves plowed under, the Gruta ranch is still a going concern, faithful to its origins and traditions.

ABOVE: *View of the Contrabandista, or Smuggler's, River. The name is current, but the illicit activity it suggests harks back to the pioneer days of colonization.*

OPPOSITE: *Like most of the ranch houses in southern Rio Grande do Sul, the great house at Gruta, built in 1853, has characteristics of Spanish colonial architecture.*

BIBLIOGRAPHY

Antonil, João Antônio Andreoni. *Cultura e Opulência do Brasil por suas Drogas e Minas* (The Culture and opulence of Brazil from its medicines and mines). Lisbon, 1711.

Auxiliador da Indústria Nacional, O. (Guide to national industry). Rio de Janeiro: Instituto Histórico e Geográfico Brasileiro, n.d.

Azevedo, Esterzilda Berenstein. *Arquitetura do Açúcar* (The Architecture of sugar). São Paulo: Nobel, 1990.

Botelho, Cândida de Arruda. *Santo Antônio.* São Paulo: Árvore da Terra, 1988.

Burns, E. Bradford. *A History of Brazil*, 2d ed. New York: Columbia University Press, 1980.

Castro, Elza Maria Vieira de, et al. *Vale do Rio Preto* (Valley of the Preto River). Valença, Rio de Janeiro: CEPA, 1988.

Dambaugh, Luella. *The Coffee Frontier in Brazil.* Gainesville: University of Florida Press, 1959.

Dean, Warren. *Rio Claro: A Brazilian Plantation System, 1820–1920.* Stanford: Stanford University Press, 1976.

Eisenberg, Peter L. *The Sugar Industry in Pernambuco: Modernization without Change.* Berkeley and Los Angeles: University of California Press, 1973.

Ferrez, Gilberto. *Pioneiros da cultura do café na era da independência* (Pioneers of the coffee culture in the period of independence). Rio de Janeiro: Instituto Histórico e Geográfico Brasileiro, 1972.

Freyre, Gilberto. *Casa Grande e Senzala.* Rio de Janeiro: Recordo, 1992. Published in English as *The Masters and the Slaves.* New York: Knopf, 1956.

———. *The Mansions and the Shanties: The Making of Modern Brazil.* 1963. Reprint. Westport, Conn.: Greenwood, 1980.

———. *New World in the Tropics.* New York: Knopf, 1959.

———. *Nordeste* (The Northeast). Rio de Janeiro: José Olímpio Editora, 1961.

Fonseca, Marta, et al. *A Fazenda São Fernando* (The fazenda São Fernando). Vassouras, Rio de Janeiro, 1994.

Furtado, Celso. *The Economic Growth of Brazil: A Survey from Colonial to Modern Times.* 1968. Reprint. Westport, Conn.: Greenwood, 1984.

———. *Formação Econômica do Brasil* (The Economic formation of Brazil). São Paulo: Editora Nacional, 1970.

Gordinho, Margarida Cintra. *A Casa do Pinhal* (The House at Pinhal). São Paulo: C. M. Knapp, 1985.

Guimarães, C. A. Araújo. *A Corte no Brasil* (The Court in Brazil). Porto Alegre, Rio Grande do Sul: Livraria Globo, 1936.

Holanda, Sergio Buarque de, and Tom Maia. *Vale do Paraíba—Velhas Fazendas* (The Paraíba valley: Old plantations). São Paulo: Editora Nacional, 1976.

Lamego, Alberto Ribeiro. *O Homem e a Serra* (Man and the mountains). Rio de Janeiro: IBGE, 1963.

———. *O Homem e o Brejo* (Man and the heath). Rio de Janeiro: IBGE, 1945.

Leite, Edgard Teixeira. *Vale do Paraíba, passado e futuro* (The Paraíba valley: Past and future). Rio de Janeiro: Carta Mensal, Confederação Nacional do Comércio, 1982.

Mathias, Herculano Gomes. *Nos Caminhos de Bananal* (On the roads of Bananal). Rio de Janeiro: Revista Geográfica Universal, Bloch Editores, 1981.

Noronha Pinto, Lourdes. *Antigas Fazendas do Rio Grande do Sul* (Old plantations in Rio Grande do Sul). Porto Alegre, Rio Grande do Sul: Grafic-Offset, 1989.

Pinho, José Wanderley de Araújo. *História de um Engenho do Recôncavo* (History of a sugar plantation on the Bay of All Saints). Rio de Janeiro: INAA, 1946.

Pires, Fernando Tasso Fragoso. *Antigas Fazendas de Café da Província Fluminense* (Old coffee plantations in Rio province). Rio de Janeiro: Editora Nova Fronteira, 1980.

———. *Fazendas—Solares da Região Cafeeira do Brasil Imperial* (Fazendas: Mansions of the coffee region of imperial Brazil). Rio de Janeiro: Editora Nova Fronteira, 1990.

———. *Antigos Engenhos de Açúcar no Brasil* (Old sugar plantations in Brazil). Rio de Janeiro: Editora Nova Fronteira, 1994.

Poppino, Rollie E. *Brazil: The Land and the People.* New York: Oxford University Press, 1968.

Porto, Luís de Almeida Nogueira. *Bananal no Império* (Bananal during the Empire). Rio de Janeiro: Editora Brasil América, 1994.

Prado Júnior, Caio. *História Econômica do Brasil* (The Economic history of Brasil). São Paulo: Editora Brasiliense, 1979.

Ribeyrolles, Charles. *Brasil Pitoresco* (Brazil in paintings). Rio de Janeiro: Tipografia nacional, 1859.

Saint-Hilaire, Auguste de. *Viagens pelas Províncias do Rio de Janeiro e Minas Gerais* (Travels through the provinces of Rio de Janeiro and Minas Gerais). São Paulo: Editora nacional, 1938.

Schwartz, Stuart. *Sugar Plantations in the Formation of Brazilian Society.* Cambridge, England: Cambridge University Press, 1986.

Silva, Eduardo. *Barões e Escravidão* (Barons and slavery). Rio de Janeiro: Nova Fronteira, 1977.

Silva, Pedro Gomes da. *Capítulos de História de Paraíba do Sul* (Chapters of the history of Paraíba do Sul). Rio de Janeiro: Brasileira de Artes Gráficas, 1991.

Simonsen, Roberto. *História Econômica do Brasil* (The economic history of Brazil). São Paulo: Editora Nacional, 1937.

Souto Maior, A. *História do Brasil* (The History of Brazil). São Paulo: Editora Nacional, 1970.

Souza Doca, E. F. *História do Rio Grande do Sul* (The History of Rio Grande do Sul). Rio de Janeiro: Organizações Simões, 1954.

Stein, Stanley J. *Vassouras, a Brazilian Coffee County 1850–1900.* Princeton: Princeton University Press, 1985.

Taunay, Afonso de Escragnole. *História do Café no Brasil* (The History of coffee in Brazil). Rio de Janeiro: Dep. Nacional do Café, 1943 (15 volumes).

———. *Pequena História do Café no Brasil* (A Short history of coffee in Brazil). Rio de Janeiro: Dep. Nacional do Café, 1945.

Teschauer, Padre Carlos. *História do Rio grande do Sul no Dois Primeiros Séculos* (The History of Rio Grande do Sul during its first two centuries). Porto Alegre, Rio Grande do Sul: Livraria Selbach, 1922.

Vellinho, Moisés. *Brazil South: Its Conquest and Settlement.* Translated from the Portuguese by Linton and Maria Barret. New York: Knopf, 1968.

Zaluar, Augusto Emilio. *Peregrinação pela Província de São Paulo* (Travels through the province of São Paulo). São Paulo and Belo Horizonte: USP-Itatiaia, 1975.

GLOSSARY

Carioca The inhabitants of the city of Rio de Janeiro are called *cariocas*. The etymological origin of the word is not entirely clear and is the subject of some controversy. In the native language *kari* means "white" and *oka*, "house," so *carioca* literally means "white man's house." The term may thus have originated from the first houses built by the Portuguese during the early days of Rio's occupation. But it may also have derived from a village of Tamoio Indians on the shores o Rio's Guanabara Bay. According to the sixteenth-century chronicler Gabriel Soares, that village was called Carioca.

Casa-Grande Throughout the sixteenth, seventeenth, and eighteenth centuries the seat of a rural estate in Brazil was referred to as the "living house." Only at the end of the eighteenth century did the term *Casa-Grande*, or great house, become widespread under the influence, perhaps, of the *grand case* of the French Antilles and the *great house* in Jamaica.

Engenho The chronicler Antonil, impressed by the complexities of *engenhos* (sugar plantations), wrote in 1711: "Whoever called the workshops where sugar is produced *engenhos* truly hit upon the proper name, because anyone who sees them and gives them proper attention is bound to confess that they are essential products and inventions of human ingenuity which, as a small portion of the Divine, always show themselves admirable in their operation."

Estância In the southern part of the state of Rio Grande do Sul, cattle fazendas are called *estâncias*, a direct influence of its Spanish-speaking neighbors.

Fazenda The word *fazenda* has several meanings, but the primary ones are "rural property" and "national treasury" (the *Ministro da Fazenda* is the Secretary of the Treasury). In the sense of a rural property it is applicable to virtually any type of rural activity, and it corresponds to *herdade* in Portugal and *hacienda* in countries of Spanish colonization in the Americas.

Fluminense Province The Portuguese word *fluminense* derives from the Lain *flumen*, or "river." During the Empire, the inhabitants of the province of Rio de Janeiro were called *fluminenses*, so that the *fluminense* province and Rio de Janeiro province are synonymous. The city of Rio de Janeiro was the principal city of the province and is now capital of the state of Rio de Janeiro. It was also the capital of Brazil until 1960, when the seat of power was moved to the new city of Brasília in the Central Highlands.

Senzala Lodgings for the slave population, *senzalas* were as obligatory on traditional sugar plantations, coffee plantations, and ranches as the great house and the barns. The term comes from the Quinbundo Indian word *sanzala*. The proximity of *senzalas* to the other buildings on the estate facilitated control over the behavior and work of the slaves. There were two types of *senzalas*: individual units and collective dwellings. Slave families occupied the individual *senzalas*, while single and elderly slaves were housed in the collective quarters.

Tulha From the Latin *tudicula*, the *tulha* was the compartment or bin where harvested coffee berries were stored after being washed and then dried on the *terreiro*, or terrace. Because the *tulha* was insulated from climatic changes, the coffee could be stored there until the optimal moment for its sale, which might not arise until the next harvest. The number and size of *tulhas* on a fazenda varied according to the volume of production. Coffee in a *tulha* was like money in a safe.

INDEX